Many Americans find money, identifying their financial goals, and planning for the future overwhelming. Jeff makes the key components of a personal financial plan accessible to all of us who are looking to be intentional and more at ease about the future. *The Eight Points of Financial Confidence* pushes you to think about what you want out of life and how you can chart a course to realize your goals. Based on over 35 years of wealth-management experience, his guidance is the perfect starting point for anyone beginning to save for the future and a nice refresher for those who want to assess their progress. It's never too early to begin building your own financial confidence!

—*Geoffrey Brown, CAE, CEO, National Association of Personal Financial Advisors*

This is among the most readable guides to personal finance you will ever find. Jeff Johnson has refined his earlier work and expanded it into a very complete guideline. There is a rule in personal finance (The Rule of 90/10) that states "...90 percent of what you need to accomplish can be done with the first 10 percent of your effort and expense." *Eight Points* is the road map to that first 90 percent, and the author gives you those valuable reference points to efficiently direct you through the remaining 10 percent. Each of the eight big pieces is taken in logical order, building on earlier information and resulting in a very satisfying trip of personal discovery. Engaging and readable, the book allows readers to easily project themselves into the various real-life scenarios presented. It is particularly helpful in conveying the value of adhering to a long-term game plan, and the author liberally sprinkles in salient anecdotes collected over decades in this profession. Very few books are both helpful and entertaining, but this is one.

—*Gerry Finnegan, CFP®*

The thinking process Jeff Johnson has gone through to create the platform, processes, and strategies of *Eight Points* is not only priceless but also worth the time you will invest in reading this book. If you do nothing else, read and complete the questions presented in the first 16 pages. If you do this, as Jeff describes, I believe your life will not only change for the better, but it will also set the course for your bigger financial future!

—*James O. Lunney, CFP®, CEP, author of* Surviving the Storm *(McGraw-Hill),* CERTIFIED FINANCIAL PLANNER™ *Professional, Certified Estate Planner, Registered Investment Advisor*

The Eight Points of Financial Confidence

Managing your life

and wealth

REVISED AND EXPANDED SECOND EDITION

Jeff C. Johnson, CFP®

Infusionmedia
Lincoln, Nebraska

Infusionmedia
140 North 8th Street #214
Lincoln, NE 68508-1353
infusion.media

Printed in the United States

10 9 8 7 6 5 4 3 2
Revised and expanded second edition

ISBN: 978-1-945834-04-2

Jeff C. Johnson
Buckingham Strategic Wealth
6940 O Street, Suite 300
Lincoln, NE 68510

The opinions voiced in this material are for general information only and are not intended to provide specific advice or recommendations for any individual. To determine which investment(s) may be appropriate for you, consult your financial adviser prior to investing. All performance referenced is historical and is no guarantee of future results.

The information contained herein is not intended to be a substitute for specific individualized tax or legal advice. We suggest that you discuss your specific situation with a qualified tax or legal adviser. Investing involves risk, including loss of principle. No strategy assures success or protects against loss.

Extreme Retirement Planning, The Three-Portfolio Approach, and The Complete Retirement Solution are trademarks of Jeff Johnson Productions, LLC.

All terms mentioned in this book that are known to be trademarks or service marks have been appropriate capitalized or otherwise specially treated; use of a term in this book should not be regarded as affecting the validity of any trademark or service mark.

Specific companies listed herein are not an endorsement of their products or services or a recommendation of any kind. They are for informational and educational purposes only.

CONTENTS

Foreword

Though Jeff C. Johnson joined Buckingham Strategic Wealth in 2017, he has been a respected investment professional since 1982. In over 35 years of on-the-job training, Jeff has gained real-world, hands-on experience that is priceless to the clients of our firm and to the readers of this book.

When Jeff asked me to review this new edition of *The Eight Points of Financial Confidence,* I happily agreed. You will find that Jeff's writing style reflects a clear voice and his heartfelt desire that the reader's life be improved as a result of this book.

The Eight Points are a logical process of thinking about your total financial picture, and the book should be read with "pen in hand" to make notes and underline the areas where the reader might be able to improve his or her financial situation.

In today's world being "financially confident" is not always easy. *The Eight Points of Financial Confidence* is a recommended first step.

—Larry Swedroe, director of research at Buckingham Strategic Wealth and author of *Reducing the Risk of Black Swans: Using the Science of Investing to Capture Returns with Less Volatility*

CHAPTER ONE

The Big Picture

You are probably reading this book because you want to know if you're "on the right track," financially speaking. Perhaps you were one of my personal finance students at the University of Nebraska-Lincoln or you read one of my books, *The Five Financial Foundations* or *The Five Financial Foundations for Physicians,* and you're ready to take your financial life to a higher level. Maybe you just want to learn if there is a better way to plan and organize your financial decisions. Like many, you are seeking a place called "Financial Confidence."

You're not alone if you wonder how you are doing financially. Having been a wealth adviser for over half of my life, I am often asked questions like "How do I know if I am doing OK?" or "Do I have enough money to educate my kids and someday retire?" or "Is there something more that I should be doing?"

Our world has no lack of financial information and mass media advice that is sometimes confusing and difficult to apply. Absorbing and using this flow of random financial data is about as practical and

efficient as drinking water from a fire hose. Piecing together bits of advice from television, magazines, internet blogs, etc., leaves many people confused, unfocused, and underconfident about their financial and life events planning.

The subject of this book is a process of systematic thinking and planning that I named the Eight Points of Financial Confidence. It is a comprehensive planning checklist that I use in my wealth management practice to advise my clients, and though it is a standardized list of questions, the answers are based on investor-client responses, making each resulting plan a unique and custom road map to Financial Confidence.

So what are the building blocks of Financial Confidence, specifically? It's knowing (or identifying) what you want out of life and how your money will support what you want to have happen; it's monitoring your progress and preserving your assets and income. Financially confident people have a repeatable investment process and an income-for-life plan in place or in progress for their retirement. They know where their money will go when they don't need it anymore (i.e., to heirs or charity). Financially confident people can often afford to be generous with charities and their heirs and to create educational funding and life opportunities for others. They also realize that, while taxes are inevitable, tax-wise strategies should always be considered when making financial decisions.

When you apply (and reapply) this Eight Point approach to your life and finances, you create your own personal financial plan. If you've grown past the "beginner stage," this planning should almost always be undertaken with an experienced and trusted wealth adviser who can assist you in developing your thinking, clarifying your true objectives, and organizing and focusing your financial assets and income to support those objectives (although there are some investors that can manage to get along without professional advice—more on that later).

Your wealth adviser should proactively help you rethink and update your Eight-Point Plan at least annually and more often if your life involves some complexities or changes.

Before moving on to the rest of the book, let's look at an overview of the Eight Points, and you can ask yourself some of the questions your wealth adviser may ask you. Jot down your answers or take note of areas that you might question, either here on these pages or on a separate sheet of paper. More specifics are in the chapters that follow.

The Eight Points of Financial Confidence

1. **Life Goals.** What do you want to have happen in your life? If we were to sit down together in three years, five years, 10 years looking back to today, what would have had to have happened in your life for you to achieve the things that are really the most important to you?

   _____
   _____
   _____
   _____
   _____
   _____
   _____
   _____

2. **Measuring Progress.** Do you have a method for periodically tracking your financial assets and income and considering how they can support your life and lifestyle? Are you using technology to monitor all of the accounts that make up your investment portfolio? Do you

have an effective way to evaluate the results of your investment portfolio?

_____

_____

_____

_____

_____

_____

_____

3. **Risk Reduction.** What financial risks can you afford to bear and which risks should you offset? Are you paying too much for segments of your risk management program? When was the last time you took inventory of your entire insurance package?

_____

_____

_____

_____

_____

_____

_____

4. **Asset Management.** Do you have a repeatable investment process in place based on your risk-tolerance levels? Are your investments managed so that they act in concert or do you have a piecemeal, unfocused portfolio? Are you investing based on hunches and projections or do you rely on academic

evidence when making and developing your investment holdings?

_____

_____

_____

_____

_____

_____

_____

5. **Life Income.** Have you created a plan for your future (or present) income for life that you know with an acceptable degree of certainty you cannot outlive?

Do you know when you can retire and how much your income will be? Should you be saving more now for your future? Have you or your advisory team developed an estimate of the probability of success for your life-income plan?

_____

_____

_____

_____

_____

_____

_____

6. **Residual Wealth.** Who or what will get your money when your time on planet Earth is past? Do you want to transfer money during your life or at life's end? Will children and other heirs get your

unconsumed wealth or will it go to charities?

_____

_____

_____

_____

_____

_____

_____

_____

7. **Education Funding.** Do you have a young person (or anyone) you would like to assist in paying for college or other vocational education? Are you using tax-efficient methods of accumulation to set this money aside? How much will you need to educate these fortunate people? Can you make a difference by mentoring someone?

_____

_____

_____

_____

_____

_____

_____

8. **Tax-Wise Planning.** What percentage of your total income goes to pay income tax? What percentage of your net worth do you pay in income tax? Do you meet with your tax professional annually (preferably in the late fall) to consider tax-wise opportunities? Will your estate

be subject to federal estate taxes or state inheritance taxes? If so, are you using tax-advantaged methods of transferring wealth? Are your investment assets positioned in a way to take advantage of the current income tax laws?

_____

_____

_____

_____

_____

_____

_____

Perhaps you've isolated one specific area where you have questions or concerns. It's perfectly acceptable to jump forward to the chapter on the "Point" where you most need to immediately apply thinking and planning. You can always return to the other chapters; there is no requirement to tackle the list in any particular sequence.

After considering the list of questions, you might realize that you need to systematically create a comprehensive plan—a financial road map. If that's the case, turn the page to the next chapter and start by identifying your destination, your most important future life achievements, and take charge of your life and wealth.

What Is a Wealth Adviser? How Do You Define Wealth Management?

Financial professionals have, over the years, worked under various titles, including financial planner, financial consultant, financial adviser, registered representative, account executive, and wealth adviser. (There are also titles such as "senior vice president" or "managing director" that are somewhat based on longevity but mostly awarded based on volume of commissions generated from the sale of investments.)

While many of the titles may sound the same, the actual services provided may vary greatly. Often the only service offered is the sale of investments or placement of money in an investment account or product. This is not what I think of as the wealth management process.

For the purposes of this book, a wealth adviser is a professional who engages in a comprehensive approach to wealth management:

- Wealth management is about investing money, but it is also about developing personal values and goals, reviewing insurance contracts and identifying uninsured risks, helping determine the need for updated estate and wealth transition plans, monitoring account progress, and educating clients on important topics that affect their financial lives.
- Wealth management requires thorough, proactive attention and collaboration between the client and the financial professional.
- Wealth management is a personal, comprehensive, and ongoing engagement between an experienced and studied financial professional and an individual who desires more than a "customer-like" relationship with a salesperson.

- True wealth advisers commit to do what's right for the client every time and accept fiduciary responsibility.

Please note: For simplicity only, in this book I will refer to wealth advisers in masculine terms, but no gender has a corner on excellence in the financial world.

I've made this book more like a workbook and fairly inexpensive. I would be honored if you would carry it in your briefcase or backpack and write all over it, make notes, underline, and identify even a few actions you can take to improve your life and impact everyone you love and who loves you.

CHAPTER TWO

Life Goals Supported by Money

LIFE GOALS. What do you want to have happen in your life? If we were to sit down together in three years, five years, or 10 years, looking back to today, what would have had to happen in your life for you to achieve the things that are really the most important to you?

It's your life. What do you want to achieve and how can money support your life goals and desired lifestyle? It's all about you. The reason we refer to our profession as "personal finance" is because it's about your finances and, well, it's personal.

"Do I really need to set goals?" you might ask. "Why not just do the best that I can and accept the outcome?"

Experience has taught me that a few people can achieve some level of success by accident, but not very many. Most of us must be intentional about making progress, both personally and financially. My time-tested advice to you is to pursue your goals on purpose. First you must identify what's really important to you.

Your goals must be *your goals*, based on your values and wishes—not someone else's thinking or society's expectations. To be valuable and attainable, there should be an emotional element (or a specific, meaningful reason) behind your desire to reach your goal or goals.

Vague goals like "I just want to invest and make money" or "I want to beat the market" foster haphazard strategies and little or no incentive to take a disciplined, pre-planned, specific plan of action.

Additionally, goals should be measurable, have a defined outcome or result, and have a time dimension to be effective. Goals that don't have a number or a due date are really just a vague wish.

Consider how these goals are the same, but different:

A. I am saving money so that I can pay college expenses for my child.
B. I am saving money for my child's college expenses because she will be the first in our family to attend college;

Goals and Future Achievements Must Be Written

In the classic book *Think and Grow Rich*, author Napoleon Hill states, "written goals are like a magnet that draws you to them." I've found this to be absolutely true, having worked with hundreds, perhaps thousands, of individuals in the development of their life plans and goals.

How you record your goals is unimportant except that they must be in writing; you can jot down notes on index cards, create a notebook, or simply refer to the financial action plan that you've developed with your wealth adviser. You can even refer to the written goals and notes you make on the worksheets in this book.

Regular review and thinking about a future life goal or goals will greatly increase the possibility of success. It's also very important to track your progress, which is the subject of the second point in the Eight Points of Financial Confidence.

I need to be able to contribute $100,000 when she enrolls in 10 years.

Which goal is backed by emotion? Which goal mentions a measureable time and dollar amount?

B certainly is the better goal; the person with goal *A* needs only to think a bit deeper, consider his or her "why," and set specific dates and times along with a specific amount. Many of the new clients we accept in our practice express unclear goals similar to *A*, so don't be disturbed if you don't have specific, measurable goals backed by emotion. You can get started exploring and identifying your true wishes in a couple of pages.

Before we move on, consider these goals:

A. I want to retire early and not run out of money.
B. I want to retire at age 55 with $5 million in savings so that I can volunteer my skills as a physician to provide care to people in need.

B is a very specific goal with a stated amount and a time frame, and it is backed up with a meaningful reason, which is the way to be intentional about setting and realizing life and financial goals.

When you discover and become aware of your true life goals, and you know what actions you must take to help realize them, you have taken a huge step toward being financially confident.

Once you've discovered a goal or goals that are important, write them down. Thoughts and feelings are fleeting and can be quickly forgotten. Writing them down makes your goals permanent and concrete.

Financial goals also require you to associate amounts of money with each goal and a timeline for accumulating the funds you need to be successful. Your wealth adviser should be helpful every step of the way by asking questions to help you discover your goals, calculating the money to support the achievement of the goal, and helping you track your progress regularly.

You can start using your imagination now and write down your goals, if you're ready.

Goal Identification and Ranking

You might already have some general (i.e., vague) goals in mind, but having just learned about the importance of being specific, time-dimensioned, and backed with emotion, you might have some thinking to do.

Consider the list of life events/goals on the next page and rank the top three to five goals based on order of importance to you. Next, rank them in the order in which you would like to accomplish them.

Importance	Order	Goal or Life Event
		Pay off debts, credit cards, college loans
		Pay off all loans, including my home mortgage
		Money for a home purchase
		Money for a vacation
		Money for the purchase of a car
		Purchase of other big-ticket item:
		Tuition payments for children, grandchildren, others
		Tuition for graduate school for yourself or a relative
		Save money for a one-year sabbatical
		Money for a newer/larger family home
		Money for a second home or vacation property
		Accumulate for retirement by this date:
		Support church or charity
		Provide funds for civic purpose
		Other goal:
		Other goal:
		Other goal:

Questions

- Can you attach an emotional reason for the achievement of your most important goals? Can you establish time frames and specific amounts of money needed to achieve these goals?
- Consider your three most important lifetime goals. Why are these important to you? How will your life change if you do NOT reach these goals?
- Which of your "urgent" goals (the goals you want to accomplish first) can you live without?

Using the worksheet on the next page, consider your top goals, determine why that goal is important to you (the emotion or strong "why"), estimate how much money it will take to achieve, decide on the due date, and state what your next step is toward reaching the goal.

You might be able to develop some calculations that can give you a starting point in estimating how much money you need as you seek to reach your goals on time.

An experienced, caring wealth adviser should proactively help you with the goal setting and realization process. Once you pinpoint, with some level of certainty, what you want to achieve in life, it's only a matter of identifying the necessary accumulation

Important Goal	Why It's Important	How Much and When	Next Step

Putting the Financial Wind at Your Back

There are really only two wealth-building engines: (1) earning money from your efforts (working) and finding ways to spend less than you're paid and (2) earning more money from your assets and investments than you spend in interest payments. The bottom line is this: When your "capital" (from net earnings and assets) makes more profit than the cost of your capital (loans, interest payments) and expenses, you have the wind at your back.

This concept often produces an "aha" moment for some high-income people when they realize that their capital is working against them, in the form of high living expenses and interest costs that are greater than their earnings.

The sooner in life that you are able to arrange your financial matters so that your pay and your investment gains are more than your living expenses, payments, and spending, the easier it will be for you to make significant financial progress toward your goals. Sometimes the defining of heart-felt goals is the motivation needed to change financial habits and get the wind at your back.

When you create your net worth statement in chapter 3, you will be able to see if your capital is working for you or against you.

and investment habits that put the "financial wind at your back."

Your wealth adviser can use his knowledge of investments and the financial world to assist you in establishing wealth-building programs. Your plan must be based on reasonable assumptions about investment returns and reasonable amounts you can save from your earned cash flow. As you develop your future directions, a "wealth analysis" can be prepared by your advisory team to give you a solid estimate of your future financial success.

To continue to expand your thinking, use the Family Timeline, a great tool to help you consider what your relationships might look like in the future. Realizing the advancing ages of your children, grandchildren, and other key people in your life (i.e., business partners, employees, other close relatives) can help you see the future with more clarity.

At my firm, an adviser might ask these questions during an initial "Discovery Meeting" with a new client:

Financial Confidence Questions to Consider and Answer during Goal Setting

1. How will money (assets and income) support your life goals and dreams? What are your most important lifetime values? How is money important to you in supporting these values?

    _____

    _____

    _____

    _____

2. How successful have you been at managing your finances in the past?

    _____

    _____

    _____

    _____

3. In which areas of your financial life would you like to see improvement?

    _____

    _____

    _____

    _____

4. There are four general ways to put the wind at your back, financially. Which of these is possible for you?
    A. Increase my income.
    B. Reduce my expenses and spending.
    C. Increase the return on my investments and assets.
    D. Reduce my cost of capital by paying off loans, lowering the amount of interest paid.

    _____

5. If you're married or in a partnership, is your spouse in agreement with you financially?

    _____

    _____

    _____

    _____

6. What's been your experience working with a wealth adviser? Will this/has this relationship helped you as you seek Financial Confidence? Should you consider upgrading the advice that you're getting?

    _____

    _____

    _____

    _____

7. What is your tolerance for investment and financial risk? How have you determined your risk tolerance in the past?

_____

_____

_____

_____

8. Who is your trusted insurance professional? How did you select him or her? Does your insurance professional work in concert with your wealth adviser?

_____

_____

_____

_____

9. Do you have a philosophy about how your investments should be managed? Do you have any "sacred" investments that can't be changed?

_____

_____

_____

_____

10. Have you considered when you can retire and what life would look like at that point? What is your vision of how your life after work will look?

_____

_____

_____

_____

11. Have you made plans for your money after your death (your "residual wealth")?

_____

_____

_____

_____

12. Do you have a trusted attorney? How did you select this professional adviser?

_____

_____

_____

_____

13. Will you be funding the education of a child, relative, or other person?

_____

_____

_____

_____

14. What are you doing to reduce taxes paid? Do you meet with a CPA or other tax professional to discuss income tax planning (in addition to the times you meet to prepare your annual income tax return)?

_____

_____

_____

_____

The Family Timeline

	Age Today	5 Years	10 Years	15 Years	20 Years	25 Years	30 Years	40 Years	50 Years
You									
Spouse									
Child									
Child									
Child									
Grand									
Grand									
Grand									
Other									
Other									
Other									

15. Can you see the value of having a "financial quarterback"? Or are you able, disciplined, and have the desire to advise yourself? Who is in the best possible position to assume this important role?

_____

_____

_____

_____

When you had no goals, no road ahead, no destination, it was difficult to feel confident about your life and your wealth. Over 30-odd years, I have been put in touch with thousands of people who had no direction, no confidence in where they were going, or had no idea what a first step might be for them. So they do little or nothing and get ... nowhere.

Now that you've targeted one or more important goals, developed some specific plans, and are starting to sense what Financial Confidence might be and where you are headed in life, you will need to monitor and

The Family Profile

Back in the day, when I was a rookie stockbroker, 30-odd years ago, I was taught Rule 405 of the New York Stock Exchange, the "Know Your Customer" rule.

Generally, NYSE member firms must obtain enough information about a new customer so that brokers can make "suitable" recommendations. Well, back in the day of buying and selling stocks and bonds, this worked fine.

Today many Registered Investment Advisory firms do so much more for clients in terms of thinking, planning, and dealing with much more complex investment offerings. Further, we accept a "fiduciary" standard (as contrasted with the "suitability" standard) that requires that we do the best thing for the client, not just selling something that is generally suitable.

To fully understand a new client, my colleagues and I use what we call the Family Profile, where we ask deep questions and sometimes uncover more complicated answers. This information is recorded on an easy-to-read and absorb chart, similar to the example Family Profile displayed on page 19.

Then, at regular progress meetings, the Family Profile is updated with new information about clients' changing circumstances. This information-gathering tool is a favorite planning component for our clients and wealth advisers.

Whether you are a do-it-yourselfer or work with a financial professional, you should have some system of regularly consolidating your financial world into a concise summary that is available for decision making.

measure your progress, the topic of the next chapter.

As you consider your financial future and what's really important to you, I recommend reading the fabulous book *Simple Money* by my colleague Tim Maurer.

The Family Profile Description

When you're a client of our wealth-management practice, we create a Family Profile. This is a wonderful tool that your wealth advisory team uses to help you explore your true feelings and most important **values and goals**.

Next, we identify your **most important relationships** and how these people fit into your plans for wealth accumulation and distribution. Whether it's children, grandchildren, or other relatives or nonfamily members, considering the future and your relationships is the foundation for most financial plans.

Your **advisory relationships** are highly important to you and to us. To maximize your results, we may need to collaborate with your legal team, your tax professionals, and your trusted insurance agent, as well as other financial specialists.

Only after understanding your goals and relationships will we assist you in inventorying your **financial assets and accounts** so that you and we can assure that you assemble a financial base that supports the goals we have discovered.

How you choose to **minimize risks** is discussed, as well as the process you prefer in working with your wealth advisory team. This includes how much contact you desire and whether it is done by telephone, in person, or through email.

Understanding an agreed-upon **process** of working together is a vital part of the advisory relationship and allows the advisory team to custom design the right mix of advice and personal contact as desired by the client.

Knowing your **interests and hobbies** is incredibly valuable in knowing you and being in a position to understand your lifetime pursuits.

Building the Family Profile and re-examining and updating this visual of your most important relationships and lifetime wishes is at the center of our firm's ongoing work as our clients' trusted wealth advisory team.

Buck and Betty Example Family Profile

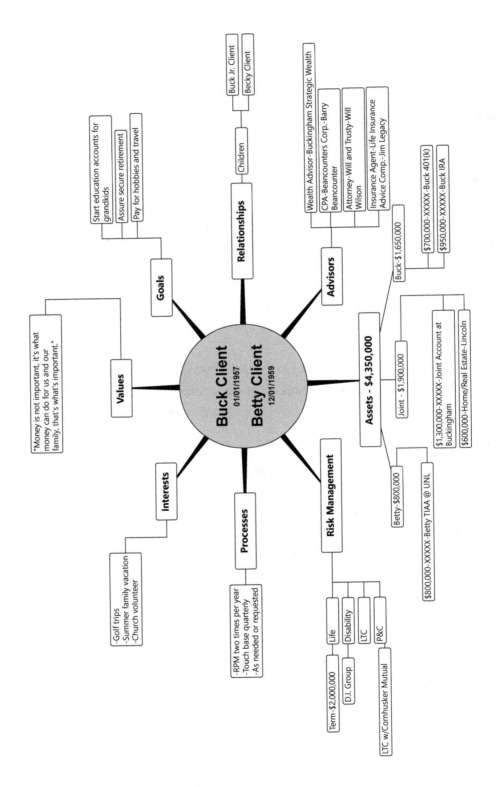

Married Money

A wealth adviser for 35 years, I am shocked at the number of new prospective clients that intend to come to my office for a first meeting without their spouse. It's often a wife that leaves "the financial stuff to my husband," but that's not always the case.

Recently, a new client came to the office with documents and statements for me to review before our first meeting. He was mildly surprised when I insisted that his wife should come to our meeting, to be part of, or at least be present for, the decision making that would take place.

Early in my career, when I didn't know better or didn't have the confidence to tell clients what I thought was in their own best interest, I often worked with the financial decision maker almost exclusively. Then, one day I would get a call from a relative, or sometimes an attorney, informing me that the decision maker had passed.

Going forward, I was unable to offer advice, help, and service that was fully trusted. During times like these, well-meaning but uninformed relatives, neighbors, and other know-it-alls come out of the woodwork to "help," often with conflicting advice or just plain bad ideas. My value to the family passed on with the decision maker.

Selecting the right adviser is extremely important because, for most people, there is just too much to know and understand in today's financial world. Just as important is to make sure that both spouses in a marriage or partners in a committed relationship understand the overall financial picture and, even more important, have a connection with a trusted financial professional that can provide incredible value during life's most stressful times.

CHAPTER THREE

Monitor and Measure Your Progress

MEASURING PROGRESS. Do you have a method for periodically tracking your financial assets and income and considering how they can support your life and lifestyle? Are you using technology to monitor all of the accounts that make up your investment portfolio? Do you have an effective way to compare the results of your investment portfolio?

Your wealth should be measured and your progress toward your desired life events and financial goals should be tracked at regular intervals. Examining your progress will encourage you to continue on during periods of strong results; periods with setbacks will motivate you to consider alternative courses of action toward new levels of success.

There's a proverb, often credited to the famous management professor Peter Drucker: "What gets measured, gets managed." I've found this to be true.

First, you should know that most people check up on their performance by casually comparing this month's statement with last month's account balance. They check to see if the values are greater, and that is that! Many investors don't even look at their statements, and unfortunately this "set-it-and-forget-it" approach doesn't fully cut it for most people with serious life and financial objectives. Having a consistent plan of monitoring your financial progress is absolutely necessary.

Also, in this day, many people never prepare—are never asked to prepare—a net worth statement that reflects their current financial position. Most lenders today simply look at verifiable income and ratios of known expenditures to make loan decisions. A net worth statement should be prepared once or twice a year by every goal-oriented person.

An income statement is another financial tool that will help you identify your net cash flow and how much you have available for discretionary spending and saving.

Your wealth adviser should proactively help you to do all of the following tasks: (a) analyze your investment account returns as well as your asset mix, (b) help you track your net worth, your total wealth, (c) project your savable income, and (d) compare your wealth accumulation to the amount needed to support your most important life goals.

Analyzing Your Investment Returns

Technology has made the monitoring of your investment accounts easy and accurate. Every wealth management firm has tools that can calculate net return for any period of time and can compare this return to market indexes. If you are not getting reports of your progress, during good times as well as during periods of decline, you should ask your financial team why.

Do take care to compare your performance to the appropriate benchmarks and for identical time frames.

If you have a moderate risk tolerance and your portfolio is 50 percent invested in growth assets with the other 50 percent in lower-risk holdings, do not expect that your results will compare favorably with an aggressive, all-stock index during strong markets. Too many media "experts" compare investment returns only to major, recognizable stock market benchmarks.

Your custom benchmark comparison should be a mix of growth and fixed-income investments that match your actual portfolio and should be developed using meaningful periods of time, not a quarter or even a single year. I recommend a minimum of

three years to evaluate and compare portfolios to a blended index.

Also, you should be aware that even a day or two difference in comparisons could have a remarkable difference in results. Investors that compare inexact periods, whether comparing to "the market" or comparing accounts against each other, can get very misleading and inaccurate data.

For example, let's say you are comparing your account at ABC Company to your investments at XYZ Firm. Be sure to use the exact beginning and ending dates and be able to factor in additions and withdrawals to the accounts. It can be very difficult to compare accurately. A trusted wealth adviser should have the tools to provide a true comparison for you.

The next section is an explanation of what a net worth statement (also called a balance sheet) is and how you can prepare one for yourself right now.

Tracking Your Asset Growth: The Net Worth Statement

There's good news when it comes to developing a system for tracking your assets and net income and measuring your progress. internet-based account aggregation services make it fast and easy to monitor your income and assets. Your wealth management firm should provide you with access to this kind of a valuable tool.

At our firm, we employ a tool that links your various financial accounts to a web page that can be viewed anytime by you and your wealth adviser. You have the ability to instantly track all of your accounts, including your company 401(k), and your investment account allocation to stocks, bonds, and cash. I encourage all my clients to use this service or something similar.

Normally one of the difficulties of creating and updating a good financial planning document is getting accurate and timely information. The tool we use and similar services should probably be considered a basic service offering of every financial planning and wealth advisory firm; back-of-the napkin doodles or estimates on a yellow pad just aren't good enough anymore.

If you're not interested in using an online service or software package, your wealth adviser should be able to assess your net worth and portfolio performance after reviewing your current financial accounts and inventorying your assets.

Your net worth is determined by making a list of everything you own (your assets, in the accounting world) and totaling that amount. Then make a list of everything you owe (liabilities) and calculate the sum of that list. Then subtract the amount you owe from the amount you own, and this gives you your net worth.

Using the worksheet below, make your own list of assets and liabilities. Do this "from scratch" in your own handwriting periodically. My experience has been that my

clients benefit with a better feel for their financial status when they take a hands-on approach every year or so.

Make a list of all the cash assets you have; then list your investment accounts, retirement accounts, and tangible assets, including the real estate you own. List anything else of monetary value, including art, stamp, or coin collections, antiques, etc. Take care to use accurate and realistic values for these items.

Next, list all of the amounts you owe: mortgage, home equity line of credit, car loans, credit card balances, etc.

The difference between your assets and your liabilities is your net worth, the measure of your wealth.

Assets (Things You Own)	
Cash	
Bank	$
Bank	$
Savings	$
Savings	$
Other cash	$
Investments	
Financial	$
Financial	$
Financial	$
Other financial	$
Retirement	
IRA	$
IRA	$
401(k)	$
Other retirement	$
Other retirement	$
Real Estate	
Home	$
Second home	$
Apartments/rentals	$
Land	$
Other real estate	$
Other real estate	$
Collectible	
Art	$
Collections	$
Personal Property	
Automobiles	$
Household	$
Total Assets	$

Liabilities (Amounts You Owe)	
Short-term Debt	
Credit cards	$
Bank loan	$
Other loan	$
Long-term Debt	
Mortgage	$
Line of credit	$
Business loan	$
Other mortgage	$
Total Liabilities	$
Net Worth	$

Recording your net worth every six months is highly recommended. Many of the clients who I work with have been keeping a record of their net worth increases for many years. It's a motivator to see your progress. Tracking progress gives you Financial Confidence.

Use the table below, or a similar form you create for yourself, to start tracking the growth of your wealth. Compare it to the money that you need to accumulate to work toward your financial objectives.

January 1, 20 _____ $ _____

July 1, 20 _____ $ _____

January 1, 20 _____ $ _____

July 1, 20 _____ $ _____

January 1, 20 _____ $ _____

July 1, 20 _____ $ _____

Your Savable Earnings: The Income Statement

An income statement reveals all of your earned income and income from other sources (i.e., investment income, payments received, etc.). This is normally pretty easy to track. Expenditures are not always as easy to identify.

The income statement is an especially valuable tool for the average investor. It shows how much you have coming in, how much is going out, and how much you're saving.

The proficient accumulator determines her savings goal and "pays herself first" by setting up automatic deposits to savings accounts, such as a cash reserve fund and 401(k) retirement plans. She then adjusts her spending and expenses based on what's available after meeting her savings goal.

Use the form on the right to determine your total income received. Calculate and subtract your total expenses from income to discover your net income available for saving based on your present spending. Then make adjustments to your expenditures and initiate a pay-yourself-first savings plan.

Average Monthly Income	
Earnings, monthly (net)	
Investments, average monthly	$
Other monthly income	$
Other monthly income	$
Total Monthly Income	$
Average Monthly Expenses	
Mortgage	$
Mortgage	$
Utilities	$
Telephone	$
Cable	$
Household	$
Insurance	$
Entertainment	$
Credit card payments	$
Cash spending	$
Other spending	$
Other spending	$
Total Expenditures	$
Net Income Available for Saving	$

Choosing Your Wealth Adviser

Proper attention to the Eight Points of Financial Confidence for a successful individual generally requires some assistance from a financial professional. Given the stakes involved, you would think most people would be very selective about who they hire as a wealth adviser. After all, this person will not only serve as a primary source of financial advice but should be experienced and able to offer a high level of life planning as well. At a minimum you would expect prospective investors would interview several wealth adviser candidates and ask them all pertinent questions about their services.

Unfortunately, this is rarely the case. Many people don't take the selection process into their own hands but rather allow the wealth adviser to choose them. They hire the first likable investment salesperson who approaches them based on appearances, with little or no "background checks" or interview.

Regardless of where or how you found a prospective wealth adviser (usually referral from a CPA, attorney, or a client of the wealth adviser), start by checking his work history at www.finra.org/brokercheck if he is a securities industry licensed person or his form ADV if he is a Registered Investment Advisor (probably posted to his website). Look for conflicts of interests or unresolved disputes.

Next, locate his website and determine what kind of organization he is affiliated with and for how long. If he is experienced and appears to have skills that you would like to employ, call for an appointment. During that call, ask if the firm or wealth adviser has an account minimum or a minimum annual fee and determine if you qualify as a prospective client. If possible, make all of your wealth adviser interviews on the same day so that you can accurately compare them.

Perhaps most important of all is to determine if the wealth adviser considers himself a fiduciary, someone required to recommend the very best solutions for you. Some investment sales organizations must only meet a standard called "suitability." Really, why would anyone want to select an adviser who isn't a fiduciary?

Here are my top 10 questions to ask when interviewing a wealth adviser candidate:

1. **How and why did you get into the wealth management business?**
   If he responds by talking about his interest in "the market" or focuses on investment products only, or can't really answer the question, you might want to move on. Stockbroker types that like to "play" with other people's money are rarely valuable advisers. A pretty good response might be "I was always good with finance and I really enjoy helping people with their money."

2. **Where and how did you learn the business of being a wealth adviser?**
   "I had sales training with my company" is not a good answer. Experience is the best teacher in most professions, and that is certainly true with wealth management; some kind of reference to experience and mentoring is preferable to only classroom or company training. Associate wealth advisers at my firm, for example, are trained through a series of in-house mentoring workshops taught by experienced wealth advisers. Additionally, associate wealth advisers work side by side with experienced wealth advisers, learning from actual client-facing situations daily until advancing into a lead adviser role.

3. **What is your process? How would we work together?** When I'm asked this question, I explain the Eight Points of Financial Confidence. My firm has a very clear client experience that every wealth adviser can readily explain to a prospective client. It starts with the gathering of client goals and resources and progresses through the recommendation stage, then to the implementation stage. Whatever it is, be sure that your prospective adviser or financial firm has a proven, successful, and repeatable process that can be put to work for you.

4. **What is your investment methodology?** You want to hear something specific, tested, and repeatable. The investments recommended should

also be tailored to your circumstances and preferences. If he says something trite like "I buy low, sell high," you might want to keep looking. Investing based on the evidence is the sensible approach that we embrace at my firm. It's surprising the number of investment salespeople that cannot articulate a consistent investment philosophy that can produce repeatable results over time.

5. **How often would you meet or communicate with me if I were your client?** Write down the responses because sometimes even well-meaning wealth advisers don't make good on their promises once they have your money under management and are earning fees. Whatever the contact system, you should feel that it would be adequate and that it would involve two-way communication.

6. **Who is going to be doing the work? Do you work alone or have a team that will serve me?** If a team is involved, ask to meet the other members and learn about their specialties or value to you if you become a client. Try to learn and understand the depth of their experience if they will be involved with your relationship. If the wealth adviser works alone, who will give you advice when he is in a meeting, away from the office, on vacation, etc.? Our clients work with a team consisting of a wealth adviser, an associate wealth adviser, and a client relationship specialist. At every planning meeting or regular progress meeting, the team meets together with our client.

7. **How much will I be involved as your client?** If you want to be part of the process, and I highly suggest that you should be, make sure the wealth adviser intends to keep you involved and can tell you his plans for your ongoing exchange of ideas.

8. **What are your fees and what, if any, conflicts do you have in serving me?** The main thing you are looking for here is full disclosure. Consider the total package, what's offered in the way of services versus the cost of the advice. Make notes so that you will remember what was said. Is your prospective firm a member of the National Association of Personal

Financial Advisors (NAPFA)? All NAPFA advisers must fully disclose fees, conflicts, and act as a fiduciary (must act in the best interest of the client at all times). Member firms must be "fee-only," which means they offer advice and are paid a fully disclosed advisory fee and must not earn commissions for a transaction or be paid for selling any product or service. There are probably many top-notch non-NAPFA advisers, but searching for a NAPFA-registered planner is probably a very good start if you are seeking solid financial advice.

9. **If I become a client and then become dissatisfied, how can I exit our relationship?** This is a very important question, if for no other reason than it immediately says about you: "I will not settle for lackluster work. If you don't follow through on your promises, I will find someone who will."

10. **Can you explain to me the first steps we would take if I decide to become a client?** Well-organized and experienced wealth advisers should have a predefined new client experience that they can explain.

Now that you've identified one or more goals and figured out how to monitor your progress, you are getting closer to a state of Financial Confidence. Next, it's time to move on to chapter 4 and consider how you can reduce or eliminate the financial risks that you and your family may not be able to bear.

Your Plan B

Your investment and financial plan should be developed based on the best estimates of future returns and the resulting probabilities. But what happens if results are actually well below historical, reasonable returns?

We know that severe declines, sometimes called bear markets, are inevitable, and we never know when or how long these periods will last.

It's important as you monitor your progress toward your goals to be aware of your "plan B," which should be a part of your Investment Policy Statement (see sidebar in chapter 5) and should be considered and documented well in advance of an actual period of market weakness.

Knowing your backup or plan B is part of having confidence in your financial future, even though difficult times may be ahead.

CHAPTER FOUR

Reducing Financial Risks

RISK REDUCTION. What financial risks can you afford to bear and which risks should be offset? Are you paying too much for segments of your risk-management program? When was the last time you took inventory of your entire insurance package?

You probably would rather not spend much time thinking about insurance, and it might be one of your *least* favorite financial decisions to consider. Believe me, you're not alone if that's the case. Still, you pay quite a few insurance premiums every year, probably several thousand dollars. This chapter is written because every financially confident person must have a well-developed wealth and asset protection plan.

Though a few people that I've known fully appreciate the need for insurance and actually seek out an insurance agent to "buy" their insurance coverage, the reality is that most people are "sold" insurance, sometimes with great reluctance. The result can be a hodgepodge, uncoordinated risk management plan, which sometimes results in gaps in your financial safety blanket.

Many of us resist the recommendations of insurance professionals, and a large number of Americans are underinsured (source: research by the Commonwealth Fund). In their minds, they are saving insurance premiums and "get away with it" by never having a loss. Unfortunately, a large, uninsured loss can financially impair that unlucky someone for life and end any possibility of reaching desired life goals.

Insurance is designed as a way for many people to sustain a reasonable and manageable loss, which is their insurance premium payment, so that a small percentage of insured individuals can be indemnified from a large, unmanageable loss. Though I've heard many claims that "insurance is a gamble," it is really the exact opposite. The insured person is trading the potential for an unknown loss for a certain and predefined loss when he pays his premium. In that light, insurance is a sure thing, isn't it? Insurance is intended to be a guaranteed and predetermined, affordable loss for most "lucky" people who never realize a large loss—hardly a gamble.

The person who avoids insurance and saves a few premium dollars could (and based on statistics, should) come out better than the person who is properly insured and paying full premium. However, the uninsured/underinsured person could suffer a huge financial setback that ruins his financial life. This is a risk that I would not recommend accepting.

Your comprehensive-thinking wealth adviser should be able to help you consider the right insurance protection for your situation, or at the very least will motivate you and point you in the right direction for advice on this important area of your financial life.

Insurance comes in different packages but generally can be divided up into two broad categories: property and casualty insurance (in the industry called "PC insurance"), which includes the protection on your home, car, and business, as well as

liability payments to others; and life coverage, which includes all life insurance and other health-related lines of protection, such as health insurance, disability, and long-term care insurance. This book is intended to assist in educating you about insurance generally and not to provide personal service. I don't take into account your personal characteristics, such as budget, assets, risk tolerance, family situation, or activities that may affect the type of insurance that would be right for you. In addition, state insurance laws and insurance underwriting rules may affect available coverage and its costs. Guarantees are based on the claims-paying ability of the issuing company. You can visit your state's insurance regulation department for more information.

Property and casualty insurance can pay you if your cars, home, real estate, or anything else of tangible value are stolen or damaged by a range of perils. Liability insurance pays "the other guy" if you do something that causes someone to suffer a loss.

Calculate Your Future Earnings as an Asset	
A. Number of years you expect to work between now and retirement	
B. Estimate of your average annual earnings for the rest of your career	$
C. Life earnings (multiply line *A* by line *B*)	$
What percentage of your lifetime earnings should you insure?	

Certainly all PC insurance is important, but for wealth-building individuals to be financially confident, it is extremely important to purchase adequately high levels of liability coverage, as they have more to lose and, unfortunately, could become targets of all kinds of lawsuits and claims, legitimate and some not so legitimate. Property losses can be big setbacks, but the large liability payment can truly ruin someone for life.

In addition to getting the maximum liability coverage on your basic automobile and homeowners insurance, you can add an additional layer of liability coverage called "umbrella" coverage, which can offer insurance protection to pay "the other guy" as much as $5 million or more (depending on your situation and your insurance company's willingness to offer the higher limits).

Take time to organize all of your property insurance paperwork, policies, etc. Ask your trusted wealth adviser to help you if you are having trouble sorting it all out, or if you just plain don't want to do it. I personally use a three-ring notebook with dividers so that I keep my auto policy and related documents behind one tab, my homeowners policy documents behind another divider,

umbrella coverage behind another, and so on. I add the new "declarations page" to the appropriate section when I get renewal forms (usually when the premium is due).

Your tabs for your PC notebook (or other filing system) could include the following:

A. Auto Owners Coverage
B. Homeowners
C. Second Home or Resort Property
D. Rental Property
E. Umbrella Liability
F. Business Owners
G. Farm and Ranch
H. Professional Liability
I. Directors and Officers Liability

While your wealth adviser should be knowledgeable about all of these insurance products, your PC professional agent should develop the details and make recommendations to you. (Can you see how having multiple PC agents could make it harder to detect a gap in your insurance protection?)

Though you may have accumulated substantial assets, if you are still working and earning money, your most valuable asset might be YOU! This is why getting the right life insurance and disability income protection is so important.

For most working people, the ability to earn is their most valuable asset, especially if they are young and talented or highly paid. Consider this: Will you earn more during the rest of your career than the current value of your investment assets and net worth? If you said yes, then your earning power is probably your most valuable asset, and you should make sure it is properly insured (especially if you have people you love and want to protect).

There are two ways to insure your earning power. The first is to secure disability income insurance to replace your earnings if you become disabled due to illness or an accident. Many employers provide coverage as an employee benefit, but normally the amount of income protected is inadequate and the period during which the benefits are paid is too short.

If your potential earnings are greater than your current investments and savings, you will want to be insured for the highest amounts, usually up to 60 percent of your eligible income. The benefit payment period, the length of time an insurance company would pay you an income if you were unable to work, should be "long term"—perhaps until age 65 or your planned retirement age.

If you and your family depend on your earnings for income, then the right disability income insurance is probably a must. And the benefits paid if you are not able to work and earn a living can be income-tax-free if you did not deduct the premiums paid for income tax purposes.

Life insurance is the second way to protect the people who depend on you if you don't live long enough to provide them with needed income. One advantage of life insurance is that the gain (the amount of the death benefit paid minus the premium paid) is income-tax-free. With proper ownership of the policy, the payment can be estate-tax-free as well (see chapter 7 on residual wealth).

There are two main types of life insurance available. Insurance that pays your beneficiaries if you die during a set period of coverage is called "term" insurance. For example, a young and healthy person can purchase term coverage for 30 years, and if he or she doesn't die during that time, the coverage ceases. This kind of life insurance is usually very inexpensive for a young buyer in his 20s or 30s and great for providing adequate protection for young families, though the premiums will increase annually and substantially over time or at the end of a set term.

"Permanent" life insurance is a lifetime contract that will pay beneficiaries when you die, even if you live to a proverbial ripe-old age. This coverage, often called "whole life," comes with a much higher but level annual premium because the company will pay the entire face amount of the policy someday (as long as you continue to pay premiums), whereas term insurance pays only if you die during the policy's term.

Financial people will often suggest that you buy term and invest the difference, meaning that you should pay lower premiums for term protection early in life, then save and invest the difference between the cost of the term insurance and the more expensive whole life. The idea is that you will have more money accumulated than if you had purchased the more expensive whole life (or other kind of permanent insurance).

In theory, this is correct thinking *if you are disciplined and able to actually save and properly invest the difference* between the lower-cost term and the whole life premiums.

On paper, term life may appear to be the better deal. Unfortunately, you don't live your life on paper. Frankly, after over 30 years working as a financial professional, I know that most people are not this disciplined. I also know that sometimes there are unexpected events that interfere with wealth accumulation plans (loss of job, health issues, divorce, stock market declines), and life insurance is still needed later in life.

I'm not suggesting that everyone should forget about term and buy whole life today, but most people should at least consider the value of establishing some amount in a permanent life insurance portfolio. If everything works out perfectly and you don't really need the life insurance later in life, you can use it as a tax-efficient wealth-transfer tool for your heirs or favorite charitable organization.

Though everyone's situation is different, most young people should purchase lower-cost term insurance very early in their working careers to adequately protect their family (or future family) from an untimely death. I suggest that this term coverage be purchased from a high-quality company that offers a nonmedical conversion to a permanent policy. This way, the young family is protected early in life, and the term insurance can be converted to lifetime coverage as career earnings rise and it becomes easier to fit higher premium payments into the family budget.

Your wealth adviser should be able to help you (or your children or grandchildren) make good decisions and can refer you to a life insurance professional who can make detailed recommendations that are appropriate.

People tend to think of long-term care insurance as nursing home insurance. I prefer the term personal care insurance because it better describes the benefits. Wealthy investors don't feel like they need personal care insurance for financial protection because they have the financial or income resources to pay without receiving insurance benefits. In recent years, it has also become much harder to qualify for a policy, with shorter benefit periods and much higher premiums than in the past.

So why do I write about personal care insurance?

First, personal care insurance is more expensive than a few years ago because

What Is a Life Insurance Professional?

The life insurance business is a very competitive and challenging sales career, and few trainees who try to make it in the field are still selling insurance five years later. Life insurance professionals are paid to sell insurance with a commission payment that is a percentage of the premiums paid. So, if you pay $10,000 per year for your life insurance, your agent might be paid $5,500 to help you make that decision (each company is a little different, but this is a reasonable example).

The decision to buy life insurance sometimes takes a very long time because it is hard to "place" due to insurance company health underwriting issues, and so requires an agent with a very strong work ethic and extremely strong commitment to serving people. A salaried salesperson would be unlikely to persist in getting the sales process completed and the proper amount and type of life insurance placed. This is why commission-compensated sales professionals are required. If you compare agent-sold life insurance and no-load, no-agent life insurance, the prices are very similar.

Your life insurance professional should be a high-integrity and experienced agent (a minimum of five years, preferably 10 years or more) who is financially successful himself. The agent with a large and busy practice (a) has demonstrated that people trust him, (b) has probably served someone like you already, and (c) is earning a good living—because of that, he has the financial ability to recommend the insurance products that are right for you, not necessarily the highest commission insurance policy that would pay him more.

A top life insurance professional is probably a Chartered Life Underwriter. The CLU designation is the widely recognized standard for professional credentials in the life insurance business. The CLU holder must stay current through an annual continuing education requirement.

Bottom line: There are a large number of people selling life insurance on a full- or part-time basis. There are only a few that are truly life insurance professionals.

Your wealth adviser should be a valuable resource to you if you want to locate and establish a solid relationship with a life insurance professional.

---

insurance companies have discovered that the claims can be substantial, potentially greater than the value of a home, an investment portfolio, or other properties. There are a number of reasons for the growing amount of claims, but in my mind there are two primary reasons for the higher benefits being paid: (1) people keep living longer and receiving insurance benefits with improving care and (2) health-care entrepreneurs keep finding ways to provide new in-home services that are covered by these policies.

Did you know that a high percentage of claims paid by companies on their personal care policies are for people who continue to live in their own homes?

Another reason that I recommend considering this coverage is because it is the "hole" in the retirement plan for many middle-income Americans. These people have an adequate (or close to adequate) amount of retirement resources, unless they need the services of a home care provider or must live in an expensive facility that will wipe out their assets.

Also, there is the issue of caregiver stress, where one spouse attempts to provide all the personal care necessary for an ailing spouse. The result is a deterioration of the caregiver's health, and both spouses then suffer from failing health.

Perhaps the most important reason that you should consider personal care insurance is not only for the financial risk it offsets but also for your family unity. Many families are divided when siblings cannot agree on the type and cost of care for aging parents. So, if you are a fairly wealthy individual, and your portfolio and income sources can pay for these services without insurance, why not pay for the insurance instead and reduce or eliminate the conflict that could damage the family relationships? Having tax-free cash payments makes the decision about how to care for you much, much easier for your spouse and/or children.

Here's how personal care insurance works:

The Activities of Daily Living

Used by health-care professionals to define skills that an individual must possess to function independently, Activities of Daily Living (ADLs) include

- Personal hygiene and grooming
- Dressing and undressing oneself
- Self-feeding
- Functional transfers (e.g., from a bed to a wheelchair)
- Toilet use
- Ambulation (walking without assistance)

You pay premiums based on the daily dollar benefit you desire, which will depend greatly on the area where you live. To offset rising costs, consider adding some kind of inflation adjustment option that will increase your daily benefits over time, effectively doubling or tripling your coverage during your retirement.

If you're unable to perform two or more of the "activities of daily living," you'll be eligible for reimbursement up to the daily limit. Services could be provided to you or your spouse as residents of an eligible facility or while living in your home, depending on the nature of your condition.

A "cognitive impairment," such as Alzheimer's, can also trigger payment of benefits—Alzheimer's is a leading cause of personal care insurance benefit payments.

My recommendation? If you do not have this coverage, start by getting a quote and balancing the cost against the amount of the potential "bucket" of money that could be paid for your care. Can you fit the premium payment into your budget? Are there people in your life you love and who love you? Understand the statistics and understand that personal care insurance benefit payments could be greater than the value of your home or even your investments. Consider how this coverage can make the lives of the people you love much easier.

The best time to contract with an insurance company for personal care insurance is (a) when you can afford it and (b) when you can qualify for the coverage (often between the ages of 40 and 55).

It's a difficult decision but one that you can make with the help of a seasoned life insurance professional and your wealth adviser.

Now that we've completed an overview of the types of coverage you might need to be financially confident, let's look at the insurance buyer's first important decisions, which are (a) selecting the right insurance professionals and (b) selecting the right companies to underwrite your risks of loss.

Property and casualty insurance and life insurance products are very different and, in my opinion, require agents in these two disciplines to possess very different skills, training, and temperament. Your PC agent (and the agent's administrative staff) should be experienced and thorough in collecting your data, inventorying your assets, and assessing your need for protection from property losses. After all, an uninsured loss can cost you dearly.

Your property agent has to deal with tangible items, such as your home, your cars, rental properties and buildings, as well as potential liabilities if somehow others are harmed by or as a result of your property or actions. PC agents need to be technically strong, understanding the insurance contracts and insurance carriers, the coverage, and the exclusions. Because lenders often require this kind of insurance, and because it's easier for people to envision a property loss, the PC agent does not normally have to be an aggressive salesperson.

Typically, your PC insurance can be changed to a different agent or another insurance company if you are unhappy with the service, or if you learn that you are uninsured in certain areas, or if you find a much lower premium for the same or greater coverage (if you have high losses or exhibit greater risk, such as a bad driving record, you might not be able to switch carriers as easily). It makes the PC insurance decision more about the right coverage and the right price.

Your life insurance agent has to be persistent, proactive, and determined because many people cannot immediately see the need for appropriate levels of life insurance, disability income insurance, and long-term care insurance. These "intangible" losses are harder for most people to imagine than the loss of property, and the premiums for some life-related insurance, especially whole life insurance, long-term care, and disability income insurance, are often substantial.

The nature of most life- and health-related products is that they are long term or should be considered long term, in some cases a lifetime. Changes in your health may make it much harder or expensive (or impossible) to switch life insurance. And consider that most people do not become healthier and lower cost to insure as they age. Usually the best price for life-related products is right now, if you qualify. This makes the decision for selecting your life-related insurance professional more important and permanent because it might cost you significantly if you and your life agent make poor choices.

It's rare that agents are really good at both property and casualty insurance and life insurance because it takes different abilities and interests. Your PC agent will know you and your property, but your life insurance professional will need to know much more about your assets, your earnings, employer-provided benefits, your family, and future plans, and he could be involved to a greater degree in your overall financial planning.

Your wealth adviser should be knowledgeable about insurance protection and will probably know professionals who can serve as your agents (and may be affiliated with a life insurance professional) if you are not already well served.

Without giving excessive detail, there are two kinds of insurance companies, stock insurance companies and mutual insurance companies. Shareholders own stock companies, and the policyholders own a mutual company.

Stock companies must make money for their stockholders, cash for dividends, and earnings that will drive the share price of the company higher. That's why investors buy shares of a company, to make money. Management of a stock insurance company has to look out for the interests of their investor-shareholders.

Stock companies might have a more uncertain future and are subject to takeovers and mergers, which can change the financial strength of the company.

Mutual insurance companies are focused on their policyholders, who are the owners of the company. Though they can "de-mutualize" and become a stock company, most mutual companies are run for the benefit of policyholders and might be less exposed to stock market events or a Wall Street takeover.

You want a financially stable company to underwrite your insurance, no matter if it is a mutual or stock company. However, the company you choose for your property insurance might be of less of an urgent concern because often this insurance protection can be changed to another company (assuming you don't have excessive losses and are a good risk for a new company to take).

Mutual companies might be viewed as steady, financially sound, conservatively run companies, especially important for long-term insurance purchases such as life insurance, disability insurance, and long-term care insurance. Once you make the purchase of life- or health-related insurance, it is likely to be expensive (or in some cases, impossible) to change, so you don't want your company to go out of business or be merged with a less financially stable organization.

The largest well-known mutual life insurance companies have very solid financial status, company-trained salespeople producing new business, and are continuing to expand the company's business, so it is likely that when you need assistance with claims or policy service matters in the far-off distant future, a nearby agency office will be available.

The largest mutual companies often do charge more in premiums than other life companies, and they have become very selective in their underwriting. This is why I teach my college students to begin building their life insurance portfolio at an early age, when they are insurable at attractive levels and prices by the best life insurance companies. (In the residual wealth chapter, I recommend the gift of high-quality life insurance to children and grandchildren as a wonderful way to transfer wealth while building something of value for the family of the young adults.)

*   *   *

The last financial risk I'll address is the problem of identity theft, which can be minimized with an amendment to some homeowners insurance policies.

According to a report by the Bureau of Justice ("Victims of Identity Theft, 2014," BJS *Bulletin*, September 2015), about 7 percent of Americans 16 and older were victims of identity theft in 2014.

About 85 percent of identity theft incidents involved the fraudulent use of existing account information, such as credit cards and bank account information. Among the victims who had personal information used for fraudulent purposes, 29 percent spent a month or more resolving problems.

In the past decade, the news media has generated lots of interest and advice—some of it helpful and some unrealistic—about identity theft. Although the threat is very real (my daughter was a victim years ago and still has to deal with lingering issues), I recommend that clients remain vigilant without yielding to paranoia. In truth, the best way to prevent identity theft is to make a habit of routinely monitoring your financial accounts for signs of mischief. Don't just pay your bills without looking at the itemized charges. Review each item to ensure that you actually authorized every charge.

In addition, you should check your credit report regularly. You're permitted to obtain a free credit report from each of the three national credit-monitoring companies (Experian, TransUnion, and Equifax) every year. Although it costs, I recommend checking your credit report more often, every four months, with each of the credit-monitoring companies. Check the reports for unauthorized charges and loans. If you spot a loan you don't recognize from a bank you've never heard of, that could be a problem; someone may have borrowed money in your name, with no plans to make payments, and eventually the lender will track you down seeking repayment of the loan.

Other signs of identity theft may include

- Unexpected phone calls from creditors;

- Being turned down for credit unexpectedly;
- Account usernames or passwords no longer working;
- Missing bills or statements.

If you suspect you've been a victim of identity theft, your first move should be to contact one of the three credit bureaus named above. Within 24 hours a fraud alert will be placed on your credit reports, alerting creditors to call for permission before opening new accounts in your name. (Unfortunately, creditors are not required to pay attention to the alerts, so keep checking your credit reports to ensure no new accounts are opened.)

Next, change all of your account access information, your passwords and logins, etc. Pick new PIN numbers for your debit and credit cards. In extreme cases you may be counseled to contact the Social Security Administration for a new Social Security number.

Contact utility companies (water, electric, gas, telephone) to let them know that an identity thief may try to open an account in your name. (Contacting phone and utility companies will also prevent an identity thief from using a bill as proof of residence when applying for new credit in your name.)

Report any actual crime committed to relevant authorizes. Call the local police department to file a report listing every fraudulent account. Get a copy of the police report and send it to the creditors and credit-reporting agencies as proof of the crime. If you suspect mail theft, notify the postal inspector. You can also complete an identity theft affidavit at the Federal Trade Commission's website and make copies to forward to creditors.

Report all fraudulent transactions directly to your creditors. Contact them for any accounts that have been tampered with or opened without your knowledge. Be sure to put your complaints in writing. Ask each creditor to provide you (and the law enforcement agencies you've contacted) with copies of the documents showing fraudulent transactions.

Lastly, make a log of all contact you make with authorities. Record each person's name, title, and phone number in case you need to recontact them or refer to them in later correspondence.

My daughter had loans taken out in her name by unknown persons when she was living in Arizona years ago. On the plus side, she never lost a dime. On the minus side, she still has to deal with the repercussions, in particular getting calls from collection agencies.

The more wealth you have, the more problematic identity theft can be because people with high net worth and good credit ratings have more to lose.

Identifying your greatest risks and offsetting those risks can only enhance one's sense of Financial Confidence. Just make sure to indemnify the large losses that you cannot handle alone.

When you're comfortable with your approach to protecting your assets and wealth, you can turn your full attention to building and enhancing your wealth, the subject of the next chapter.

CHAPTER FIVE

Investments and Asset Management

ASSET MANAGEMENT. Do you have a repeatable investment process in place based on your risk-tolerance levels? Are your investments managed so that they act in concert or do you have a piecemeal, unfocused portfolio? Are you investing based on hunches and projections or do you rely on academic evidence when making and developing your investment holdings?

There are whole industries built on the notion that you can "beat the market" or that there is a smarter guy or a secret sauce to making money investing in the equity markets. Working for four decades has taught me by observation that this is not true, over time. Real people who have made money investing for the long haul used commonsense buy-and-hold approaches, with some modest rebalancing periodically.

To be clear, really good investment strategies are boring. I repeat for emphasis, they are boring.

Boring doesn't always sell, so innovative vendors of investment products work to find ways to appeal to greed and vanity by proposing a new, better idea by the smartest guy or firm.

Many new and creative investments packaged by Wall Street's marketing machine have sizzle and a strong appeal. Sometimes these hot ideas seem to have greater immediate potential than commonsense strategies based on actual evidence. On closer examination, these sometimes unproven investments or strategies often have high expenses, assume substantial risks, and are managed in a highly aggressive manner, yet yield modest results or can even lose money, like any other investment.

Assuming you are more interested in outcomes than adventure, long-term investments in diversified stock holdings have produced attractive results, historically speaking.

If you have defined your life goals and have reasonable time frames to build the financial assets to support those goals, a high-single-digit return over multiyear periods may be an adequate return, I believe. If you are young or someone who can

40 Years × 10% = 45×

Money compounding at 10 percent per year multiplies more than 45 times in 40 years. If you are in your 20s, you can make a $1,000 investment, and if you can earn an average of 10 percent over that 40 years, your investment will grow to $45,000. Saving $5,000 today would grow to $225,000 based on these assumptions. (Note: While historically reasonable, I am not guaranteeing 10 percent returns! This is a hypothetical example and does not represent an actual client's experiences.)

commit to a long-term investment portfolio that is growth-only invested, perhaps 10 percent per annum is possible over a long stretch of time, and by long term, I mean 20-plus years to see substantial results. Although you can't invest directly in an index, if you examine the historical evidence of equity returns, I think you might agree that 10 percent could be achievable.

A common obstacle is a lack of long-term thinking. The news media, including financial media, are in business to deliver a story today, driven by tight deadlines and a desire to find stories that sell—stories that will prompt people to buy newspapers, click hyperlinks, and glue their eyes to television broadcasts (and the advertisements that pay reporters' salaries).

Drama sells. Conflicts and short-term worries sell.

Steady progress over periods of years is boring.

Today, our society benefits and suffers from an information surplus. Some of the information is valuable and helpful; some of the information is harmful. Here's a real-life example:

A young farming couple came to see me (I think age 55 is young) for guidance on what to do to improve their financial circumstances. They had taken a retirement planning class that I taught at the local community college and scheduled an appointment to meet with me. After reviewing their situation, I found they had substantial free cash flow that was fully taxable and could set up a pension plan, saving and deducting over $100,000 per year, as well as boosting the return they were earning on a very large chunk of cash. This action would have been a small step toward a more diversified asset base as they neared retirement.

Later, they called back to thank me for my time but had decided to "stay put." After watching the news, they said, "The stock market is so wild that we're afraid to invest in it, and instead we've decided to buy more farmland." In other words, they planned to diversify by buying more farmland at all-time-high prices because they focused on short-term thinking.

This is an example of the news media scaring people away from a long-term course of action that could have been very beneficial for them.

Taking advantage of the long-term growth opportunities offered by investments in stocks does not have to be difficult. It does require long-term thinking and focusing on the distant future.

Here's the four-step method that I recommend and actually use (and reuse) with clients that I work with.

1. **Discuss and carefully define in a written "Investment Policy Statement" what it is that you want to achieve.** Having read and considered chapter 1 of this book, this should be fairly straightforward. If you're a young person just starting out on your financial journey, your goals might include building wealth that will be used to support your family, buying a future home or business, or educating children. If you are nearing the end of your working career, you might be interested in creating lasting (and growing) income by investing money you accumulate from the sale of property or your business or from a retirement plan. Wealthy investors might want to enhance their returns so that they can provide larger sums of money for transfer to family or charity. Be sure you are clear on what you are seeking to achieve and write it down so that you can stay on track. (See examples from an Investment Policy Statement, pages 54–60.)

2. **Next, determine your tolerance for risk and volatility.** Publicly traded stock investments can and will fluctuate; sometimes the declines can be breathtaking. If you own stock investments, it should be through low-cost, institutional-quality portfolios, and you should absolutely be prepared to withstand declines of 20-30 percent or more. Sometimes prospective clients will tell their adviser to call them or get them out when it looks like the market is going to decline. Well, based on the historical evidence, this is not possible to do, at least not with any consistency. The price for the attractive potential returns of owning stock investments is that you must be long term in your thinking and you must be willing to withstand drastic price movements. Consider this: How much decline in your total portfolio can you stomach?

Diversification within the Equity Asset Class

Portfolio Three is usually composed of stock mutual fund investments, but selecting equity holdings within this asset class that have very different characteristics can enhance diversification and boost investment returns.

For example, holding a percentage of stock investments in large US companies will "track" very closely with the major, well-followed US indexes, such as the Dow Jones Industrial Average or the S&P 500. A well-diversified portfolio could also be invested in small companies that, while little known, offer higher returns but with greater volatility. Non-US companies are often added to equity portfolios to further diversify the results.

A seasoned wealth adviser will have a firm philosophy that can quickly be articulated when you ask about it.

Your Investment Policy Statement (see sidebar on page 54) should describe your diversification plan in detail.

If you can withstand declines of 30–50 percent, you can probably hold significant percentages of stocks in your portfolio. If, on the other hand, you think you can only tolerate a decline of 10 percent, then you should own a modest component of stock investments, maybe 25–30 percent of your portfolio. A seasoned, market-wise wealth adviser will help you think carefully through this important allocation decision and assist you in setting an asset mix that is right for you. All of this should be incorporated into your Investment Policy Statement.

3. **Think of your investments as "three kinds of money" (the Three-Portfolio Approach):** The money you need within the next year; the money you need during an intermediate period of time, say, eight to 10 years; and the money that can be left invested, no matter what happens to temporary stock prices, for over eight to 10 years (and preferably for 20 years or more). Here's how to think about it conceptually:

Portfolio One (P-1) is the place where you "bank" money that you will need in the next 12 months. This is the money you will live on if you're no

Potential Returns, Predictability, and Anticipated Holding Period Are All Related		
Potential Returns	Predictability	Holding Period
High (equity)	Low	Long (8 years minimum)
Moderate (fixed income)	Moderate	Intermediate (2–8 years)
Low (cash)	High	Short (1 year or less)

longer earning a paycheck; this is the money that will pay expenses you have due in the next year. The proper investment for this corner of your portfolio is cash, or something that matures during this period. So liquidity, availability, and an absence of risk are the right choices for this money (even if the investment return is very small).

Portfolio Two (P-2) is the money you will need in the period from one year from today out to eight years from today. If you are retired, you will want to have a "laddered portfolio" or some predetermined stream of income to meet your needs. If you have obligations that will need to be paid—balloon payments, college education bills for your youngster, a dreamed-of summer-long vacation, etc.—you will want to have investments that will mature or be readily available to meet those requirements. The main reason to hold fixed income is to reduce volatility and provide reliable cash flow, therefore fixed income should be of very high quality and due to mature in five to eight years, depending on yields at the time of purchase.

Portfolio Three (P-3) is the money that you can invest for at least eight years. This is the portion of your money that can seek long-term growth and be subject to fluctuations in value. Because you have your cash flow needs covered for the next year with P-1 and your need for income in years two to eight locked in with P-2, you can better hold your stock investment through the inevitable market declines you will experience. Just to be clear, you can be almost certain that a dramatic decline in value will occur during just about any eight-year period. (Though there have been a few exceptions, let's not plan on it.)

Using this practical, repeatable approach will help you and your wealth adviser allocate your assets between stocks, bonds, and cash in a manner that serves your needs and is not based on some mystic formula involving your age or some other method of magically getting the right amounts invested in these asset classes.

Changes in your portfolio should be based on your needs for income and

The Basics: What Is a Stock? What Is a Bond? What Are Mutual Funds?

Owning a share of "stock" means that you are the owner of a piece of a specific company. Whether you own one share, 100 shares, or millions of shares, you own the exact same thing, except the amount or percentage of the company that you own depends on the number of shares. Shares of publicly traded companies can be bought and sold by investors. This drives the prices up and down, depending on the supply of stock for sale by shareholders that want to reduce their holdings and the demand for the shares by those who want to accumulate more stock. The daily price of the stock, therefore, is determined by the perceived value of people willing to buy or sell the shares. There is no guarantee of what the value will be, except that the shareholder has this legal claim on the "equity" of this company.

A bond is a certificate that is evidence of an amount due from the company, or in the case of government bonds, a city, county, school district, state, the federal government, or some other political subdivision. The bondholder is really a lender to the entity and is entitled to interest and principal payments due as described on the bond certificate or other legal document assigned to the bond. Publicly traded bonds are bought and sold by investors and are liquid in varying degrees. The price is determined by supply and demand, just like stock prices; however, the primary impact in the change in price of a bond is the movement of interest rates and changes in the credit quality (the ability of the issuer to pay interest and principal when due). Generally, bond prices decline when the prevailing interest rates rise; bond prices rise when interest rates decline.

A mutual fund is an investment that pools the money of many investors —its shareholders—to invest in a variety of securities. Investments may be made in stocks, bonds, money market securities, or some combination of these.

For the individual investor, mutual funds provide the benefit of diversification, or by holding in many different securities that might not otherwise be available or affordable.

Professional investment managers choose the securities for the fund and manage the portfolio on an ongoing basis.

growth, not on guessing what the stock market is going to do.

At my firm, we use a powerful, computer-based tool called a wealth analysis that helps us understand our client's **ability**, **willingness**, and **need** to take risk, and then guide the client to take only the risks necessary to meet his or her goal.

If a client has many years to accumulate money and actually needs a high long-term return, then a larger component of the portfolio goes to the long-term growth investment. However, if a client has realized most or even all of the money needed to meet retirement and wealth-transfer goals, why take on significant risks?

Additionally, your adviser should pay attention to taxwise asset allocation of assets based on your financial situation and the income tax treatment of various investments you own. More on this tax location strategy in chapter 9.

4. **Reassess your portfolio and your goals regularly and make adjustments if necessary.** Every investor should be sure that their portfolio reflects their tolerance for uncertainty in short-term values (i.e., volatility). Sometimes changes in goals and hoped-for outcomes require a change in investment holdings. This does not mean that you should become more conservative or aggressive based on current market conditions. Common sense says "buy low, sell high," but human nature silently screams, "sell low" (when the news is bad and prices are down) and "buy high" (when the news is favorable and prices have already gone up). A market-wise wealth adviser can earn his pay by helping clients navigate the perils of reactionary behavior. The previously discussed Three-Portfolio Approach can help investors and their advisers see how money and a portfolio can be shaped to meet an individual's unique needs for income, growth, and cash for spending.

Time, Risk, and Reward Potential: Using the Three-Portfolio Approach

When I am asked to help a client make an investment choice, I immediately ask, "What will this money be used for, and when will you need this money?"

If the money is needed within 12 months, it must be invested in **Portfolio One**. This is for short-term investments only, highly liquid products that could have no or low penalties and have historically lower risk. Notice that nothing was mentioned about the return.

Should money be invested for a purpose that will occur in the next eight years, but more than one year out, it should go into **Portfolio Two**. This is money that can be readily available between one year from today and eight years from now with investments in bonds, notes, and securities instruments that will mature during that period, when needed.

Longer-term investments of eight years or more should be invested in ... you guessed it, **Portfolio Three**. This is the money that could be invested in higher-growth potential, higher-volatility, and less predictable investments.

So let's do a hypothetical example that could reflect a real-life situation.

You have $100,000 in cash that you have available for investment. Should you put it in stocks, bonds, or cash? Well, the answer is probably all of these asset classes, but how much? Well, we need to know more, don't we?

So, we ask, "What is the money to be used for, and when is it needed?" We discover the following.

The money came from property sold at a gain, so we need to hold out $10,000 to add to our income tax payment. Another $40,000 is needed to pay tuition for a child that is headed to college in three years. The balance of $50,000 is money not needed in the foreseeable future, probably not until retirement.

How should this money be invested (i.e., allocated)?

Portfolio One	$10,000	For the tax payment due
Portfolio Two	$40,000	For college tuition, more than one but less than eight years
Portfolio Three	$50,000	For long-term investment, probably to be used in retirement

See the chart "Potential Returns, Predictability, and Anticipated Holding Period Are All Related" on page 49.

There are many investors today that contemplate doing it themselves and making investment choices without the services of a wealth adviser or other financial professional. I'm often asked what I think about that approach.

Frankly, there are some people who are certainly capable of making their own investments. Based on my 30-plus years actually working with real people on an almost daily basis, I can tell you that most individuals need some assistance, and many need to have all investment decisions made for them by a professional.

Consider these questions:

1. If you've already been investing on your own, how is it going?
2. Do you have a process that has been working?
3. Are you comfortable making periodic decisions about what to buy and sell?
4. How are you assessing your own tolerance for portfolio risk and volatility?
5. Do you have the time to devote to your portfolio and the continuous learning that is required to be a successful investor?
6. Do you enjoy investing and managing your own money?

If you're doing great, why make a change? Still, after years of having the media and discount brokerage advertisements tell the public to "do it yourself," my colleagues and I are often connected with people who are disappointed in DIY investing. Knowing they can do better, they are much like the man who recently sent me an email saying, "I'm tired of fumbling around with my serious money without making progress or really knowing what I am doing."

So, how are you really doing? If you feel good about your results, keep it up. If you're

The Investment Policy Statement

The Investment Policy Statement is your (and your wealth adviser's) guide to how your account will be managed. Though there is no set requirement, and most Registered Investment Advisors develop their own document, following is a high-level view of a sample IPS.

The Introduction overviews the financial planning and investing process, developing goals, assessing risks, outlining specific investment strategies, and how the investments will be kept up-to-date and compliant with the IPS.

The nitty-gritty of the portfolio development should be carefully and clearly stated, and the portfolio asset allocation targets should be displayed. This sample portfolio sets the asset mix at 50 percent equity (i.e., stocks), 15 percent nonstock market ("alternative") growth investments, and 35 percent in fixed income (bonds).

At my firm, we realize the importance of helping clients understand their ability to take risk, their willingness to take risk, and their need to take risk, as well as the historical performance of a portfolio similar to their stated asset mix.

More detail about the investments and the composition of the portfolio paint a complete picture of the strategies and approach that will be used to manage the portfolio.

Not to be skipped over, the advisory fees paid by the client to the firm are clearly stated. At the end, the client and adviser sign to attest to their acceptance and agreement.

The following pages show portions of a sample Investment Policy Statement for the imaginary "Buck and Betty."

Investment Plan and Investment Policy Statement

for Buck & Betty Client

April 13, 2018

Buck and Betty Example Investment Policy Statement (continued)

Your Recommended Broad Asset Allocation

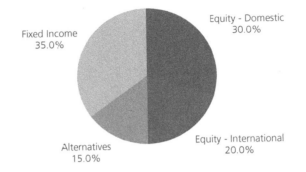

Additional Information:

Related Constraints (if any): No known constraints.

Buck and Betty Example Investment Policy Statement (continued)

Allocation and Rebalancing Guidelines

Asset Class	% of Portfolio		
	Min	Target	Max
EQUITY			
Domestic Equities			
TOTAL DOMESTIC EQUITIES	25.0	30.0	35.0
International Equities			
TOTAL INTERNATIONAL EQUITIES	15.0	20.0	25.0
TOTAL EQUITY	45.0	50 0	55.0
TOTAL ALTERNATIVES	10.0	15.0	20.0
FIXED INCOME			
Fixed Income - (Nominal, TIPS*, Cash)	30.0	35.0	40.0
TOTAL FIXED INCOME	30.0	35.0	40.0
TOTAL		**100.0**	

* Treasury Inflation Protected Securities

Buck and Betty Example Investment Policy Statement (continued)

Risk Assessment

Ability to Take Risk
Your ability to take risk is most commonly a function of the time horizon of your investment objective. Longer time horizons argue for more aggressive asset allocation strategies, since a long time horizon gives the portfolio more time to recover after periods of poor performance.

Willingness to Take Risk
Willingness to take risk measures your tolerance for risk. Specifically, we attempt to measure the amount of portfolio loss you are capable of experiencing without it significantly affecting your quality of life or causing you to change portfolio strategy.

Need to Take Risk
Your need to take risk is related to how much wealth you have accumulated, how much you expect to save and how much you expect to spend. Need to take risk is high for investors that expect to withdraw (or are withdrawing) a relatively high proportion of their investment portfolios to fund living expenses.

Tracking Error Risk
Some investors are sensitive to how their portfolio performs relative to well-known U.S. stock indexes like the S&P 500. While we encourage you not to constantly compare portfolio returns to benchmark returns since it can lead to counterproductive, returns-chasing behavior, we nevertheless cannot ignore the tendency for some investors to make this comparison. The two primary sources of tracking error in the portfolios we customarily build for clients are allocations to international and emerging markets stocks and tilts toward small-cap and value-oriented stocks.

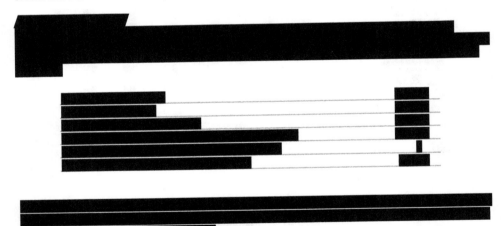

Buck and Betty Example Investment Policy Statement (continued)

Your Asset Location

We will look to place less tax-efficient asset classes like alternatives and fixed income in tax-advantaged accounts. Over time, this will help reduce your tax burden and consequently improve your after-tax return. It also means that each account will not be allocated the same; some asset classes may be held in one account but not in others. Focusing on achieving the *overall allocation* in a tax-efficient manner is the reason for this approach.

Based on the information you provided, the table below shows the initial recommended location of your assets. These locations were carefully considered to ensure appropriate continuity and to further improve the tax efficiency of your portfolio.

Initial Recommended Asset Location

	Equity	Alternatives	Fixed Income	Total
Taxable Account				
Buck and Betty Joint	$1,000,000	$0	$300,000	$1,300,000
Tax-Deferred Account				
Buck IRA	$0	$300,000	$400,000	$700,000
Tax-Free Account				
Totals	$1,000,000	$300,000	$700,000	$2,000,000
% of Total	50%	15%	35%	100%

Buck and Betty Example Investment Policy Statement (continued)

Investment Advisor Fees

Our investment advisor fees are deducted quarterly in advance from your account as follows:

Fees are computed and billed quarterly, in advance, and are based on the market value of Client's Account on the last day of the month in the prior quarter. Fees will be prorated, on a monthly basis, with respect to new Accounts opened during a quarter.

Individual Accounts for immediate family members (such as husband, wife and dependent children) are aggregated, and the fee is charged based on the total value of all family members' accounts.

not that thrilled about your own investments or are working with a professional with less-than-adequate results, consider interviewing a new advisory team. As you mature as an investor and your wealth and investment assets grow, mistakes are more painful and difficult to recover from, and time is not on your side.

OK, you've developed some thoughts about your future life and the road to your destination. You're able to understand tracking and monitoring your progress, and you have big risks (like a big medical bill, your house burning, getting sued for a bundle) covered by an insurance company. You have a good sense of how to invest money, or at least how to take a first step to building wealth; your feeling of Financial Confidence is growing! You're ready to keep increasing your feeling of well-being and continue to consider your future.

One of the greatest financial planning and investment needs in America today is orchestrating the conversion of wealth accumulated over a working career into income that will hopefully last for life (the subject of the next chapter).

Investment, Risk, and Return in the Market

When Average Isn't Average

It goes to reason that the "average" stock mutual fund would generate investment results equal to the return of a market index such as the S&P 500 index or the Dow Jones Industrial Average. But it's not true.

To be very clear, the average actively managed mutual fund does not beat the market averages. In fact, statistics reveal that most mutual funds cannot beat the index* that measures their asset class.

Most large company mutual funds that are widely diversified in US companies cannot beat the well-known S&P 500 stock index. In a typical year about one out of six mutual funds that own the largest companies' stock actually outperform the index. And that group of outperformers changes most years!

Well, shoot, that's a bummer, you might say. But is it really?

Historical, long-term returns of stock indexes have generated attractive returns. Why not seek market average returns for starters, then boost returns by overweighting smaller companies and "value" stocks, the sectors of the equity market that boast the highest long-term returns? Additional returns can be realized by reducing the internal investment costs, which increases net return.

An important point that many investors (and some advisers) never learn: **Mutual funds designed to match the return of a stock index beat the majority of similar mutual funds.**

This is where "average" is better than average.

The Efficient Market Hypothesis versus the Smartest Guy in the Room

The Efficient Market Hypothesis, in its simplest form, says that the market prices immediately adjust to an accurate price due to the dissemination of information into the market. The result is there is never (or rarely) a mispriced stock because all prices reflect the current environment and news. Among financial academics there is an ongoing debate about the EMH, but there are facts that are hard to ignore: The majority of money managers do not outperform an index that measures the asset class that compares to the manager's portfolio.

Conventional wisdom is that the market is inefficient and that smart people can "outsmart" the market. Let me just come right out and say it: There is no smarter guy in the room. I've been a financial professional for well over 30 years. I know hundreds, if not thousands, of investment people, and I've never seen the person who is consistently a top performer. There may be that one-in-a-million stock-picking genius—there have been a scarce few in the past, and I imagine there will be some in the future—but we never know who they are until later. History and the evidence suggest that it's impossible to find them before they demonstrate their proficiency, except for random luck.

As a wealth adviser, a way to high returns potential is to make sure clients are as aggressively invested as possible for as long as possible because, over time, stocks will likely have outperformed bonds and other investments. The downside is that many clients who were happy when markets were rising will inevitably sell out when a big decline in values comes (and it always does), leaving them with a permanent loss, even if the market decline was temporary. These people are better served by a portfolio that has a risk and volatility profile more in line with their temperament and tolerance.

An overwhelming majority of investment managers do not outperform a market index that measures the results from a defined asset class applicable to their investment style. In many asset classes, only 10–20 percent of investment managers can beat the index in any single year, let alone consistently for years and years.

As a professional entrusted with millions of investment dollars to advise, my rationale is this: "If I can diversify my equity holdings by asset class, and consistently perform in the top half or quarter of all investment managers in these areas, over time, my clients (and my own money) may likely achieve attractive returns with acceptable levels of volatility and absolute risk."

There are indexes that measure the return of various asset classes that have different return and risk characteristics. For example, large US companies will likely have much different results than companies from developing economies or small US companies, etc. Proper measurement of stock market returns should be based on comparisons to an appropriate index. Measuring small company or international investments to the S&P 500, which is made up of large US companies, is a faulty comparison. Likewise, comparing a well-diversified portfolio to any one index can lead to poor decision making.

Making Money in Stocks

How do you make money in stocks? Some will say you buy low and sell high, using a trite phrase offered with a simple grin.

But in fact, what do people do, especially unadvised investors? They buy high and sell low because they react to their "gut instinct," which is almost always wrong in the long run.

How does this happen?

It's easy to follow the crowd, to initiate and add to investments when the news is all good and the strong economy and recent profits in stocks make confidence levels high.

Then, the news is grim, the economy is soft, stock prices turn downward, and the paper profits in the account disappear, and the gut instinct screams to the brain, "Don't just sit there, do something." And the only thing to do is sell for a loss.

The problem with getting out is knowing when you get back in. It means you have to be right on the decision to sell, and then if values actually do go lower, you have to pick a point, and act, and get back in. It sounds simple, but it's not easy.

A better plan is to build the right balance of stock mutual funds and fixed income and

The Six Important Aspects of Buckingham's Investment Strategy

These characteristics are the solid foundation of a repeatable process built on a foundation of academic research and backed up by real-world practitioner results.

1. We invest based on the evidence that the Efficient Market Hypothesis does work and build on academic research. Using structured asset class mutual funds, principally from Dimensional Funds Advisors, we build low-cost equity mutual fund portfolios.

2. By overweighting or "tilting" the portfolio toward the highest-expected return asset classes, we increase the volatility but also the long-term expected return. This allows many investor portfolios to reduce the overall exposure to stock market-based investments.

3. The evidence is conclusive that long-term investors should overcome "home-country bias" and invest globally for the benefit of diversification as well as potentially greater return, over time. Note: Nearly half of the world's equity market value is composed of non-US stocks.

4. Because the portfolio is tilted toward equity investment with greater return potential, as well as increased volatility and unpredictability, the need for a secure bond or fixed-income portfolio is certain. We use bonds to anchor the portfolio for the unknown financial storm that lingers in the future and use the highest-quality fixed income investments.

5. Additionally, to reduce risks and increase stability of portfolio values, only shorter-term bonds are selected for the portfolio based on the client's need. Consideration is given to bond yields based on the length of time until the bond matures.

6. Using tax-wise "asset location" enhances the long-term, after-tax return of a portfolio and in some cases is significantly different than many people are actually invested.

If you are managing your own money, you should have a clearly articulated philosophy that is repeatable and built on evidence, not on guesses about the future. Likewise, any investment management or wealth advisory firm should be able to share with you their proven approach to investing money.

plan on permitting this portfolio to work for you for many years; in fact, a couple of decades will likely yield the best results.

Should You Have More or Less Invested in Stocks?

Deciding how much you have invested in stock mutual funds rather than in more secure investments like bonds or CDs is an important decision and the primary determinant of your expected long-term investment returns.

Listed are some of the reasons you could hold higher levels of equities. Consider the following with your wealth adviser:

1. How long can you leave the money invested? Do you have a long career ahead and can you wait out a difficult stock market? Can you wait for recovery before needing your invested assets? Are you familiar with the history of stock market returns?

2. How steady is your income? If you have a very secure position and fixed salary, perhaps you can tolerate more uncertainty of income than the commissioned salesperson or business owner who has unpredictable income. Some retired people have substantial fixed income from pensions, rental income, and Social Security and can patiently hold equity investments.

3. How confident are you as an investor? Some people just have a higher comfort level with risk and are OK waiting out market declines. Others get nervous and need to "relieve the pressure" by selling for a permanent loss.

4. Is there a reason you need or want higher returns? Sometimes identifying a valid, heartfelt goal makes the holding of stocks over the long term easier than for

Larry Swedroe, the Author

My introduction to Dimensional funds, Buckingham Strategic Wealth, and Larry Swedroe came in 1998 when a copy of Larry's first book fell into my hands. At this point I had been a financial advisor-stockbroker for over 16 years, and as I read this book one snowy Sunday afternoon, I intuitively knew his thinking was absolutely the right way to invest. And it still is.

Fast-forward nearly 20 years, and here I am, a wealth adviser with Buckingham and proud to be an associate of Larry Swedroe, then and now the director of research at Buckingham Strategic Wealth.

In this chapter on investments, I focus on the practical approach to investing, the best way that you can work with a wealth adviser, and strategies that you can implement.

Intentionally, I have not dug down into the investment nitty-gritty because Larry Swedroe has done that with his books, now numbering 15 works. I've read them all, and if you love to study and consider financial matters, markets, and statistics, you should, too.

If you want a great weekend read, pick up a copy of Larry's book *Think, Act, and Invest Like Warren Buffett*. For a deeper dive into the latest research, read *Your Complete Guide to Factor-Based Investing*, a book written with Dr. Andrew Berkin. Or to capture that initial inspiration I found in 1998, read *The Only Guide to a Winning Investment Strategy You'll Ever Need*.

---

the person who doesn't have a strong desire or reason for wanting greater wealth. For example: I want to leave a large legacy to my college or university.

5. Do you have other options or a "plan B" that can allow you to accept more risk or uncertainty of results? Consider the person who wants more stock exposure with the desire to retire earlier but is willing to extend his working career if the markets don't cooperate with the retire-early plan.

Increasing Investment Return Potential by Increasing Exposure to "Three Factors"

Professors Eugene Fama and Kenneth French, in an article in the *Journal of Finance* (June 1992), describe how risk and portfolio return can be explained by exposure to three factors:

1. Investment in the equity markets versus holding cash or other "no-risk" assets,
2. Smaller companies versus companies with large market capitalization, and
3. Value stocks (characterized by high book-to-market stocks) versus growth stocks (low book-to-market stocks).

By overweighting or "tilting" a portfolio toward these factors, investment returns can be enhanced over meaningful periods of time (i.e., 20 years or greater).

Your Sleep-at-Night Portfolio

When we talk about investment risk, what are we talking about, really?

In my early career, if you only owned a few individual stocks, bad market declines and a bad economy could lead to a total or near-total loss of capital. The risk of permanent loss was potentially a very great percentage of the money invested.

Owning a handful of individual stocks can lead to superior performance in the short term if you are right (or lucky). Still, other investors that have tried this approach have had to overcome loss of capital when the "business risk" of a company caused it to lose a lot of value or go out of business completely.

A properly diversified mix of institutional-quality mutual funds takes that *business risk* down to a very, very low level. What are the chances that all of the stocks held in your combined mutual fund portfolio (probably over 10,000 individual stocks within a few diversified funds) will go out of business?

So, when we talk about risk in your diversified mutual fund portfolio, what are we really talking about? *Market risk* is more about uncertainty, unpredictability, and the possible requirement that you hold onto stock mutual fund investments that are "underwater" or reduced in value for what seems like an agonizingly long period of time (usually a year or two, but possibly much longer).

The price for historical equity market returns seems to be the pain that is felt when markets are in decline for long periods of time. And to be absolutely clear, there will be significant stock market declines in the future. It is inevitable. We know there will be bear markets; we just never can really know when or for how long they will last.

Your wealth adviser should be helping you assess that risk and building a portfolio that will permit you to sleep at night. This portfolio should probably be composed of mutual funds that own stocks and

What Do You Think about the Market?

People have been asking me this question since 1982, when I passed my test to become a "registered representative" with a regional stock brokerage firm, a member of the New York Stock Exchange. Though my firm had an exceptional training program, I really didn't know very much as a 25-year-old rookie stockbroker.

Still, the Dow Jones Industrial Average was about 777 at that time, and as of this writing it is over 23,000! If I had consistently recommended to buy diversified portfolios of mutual funds and always convinced clients to "hold on" and to "add more" when the market was in decline, think of the wealth that would have been created!

I don't have to use much imagination because I still work with a number of clients from the 1980s that did just that, and every workday I get to realize some satisfaction as I observe their results.

So, what about today? It's 35 years later. Stock prices are at or near an all-time high. What about the market now? Is it too high? What about all the news, the turmoil in the world, and the media warnings to get into cash?

Recently, some very smart prospective clients have told me they think that the market is overvalued. They cite all the reasons in the previous paragraph and even more. "It's all gone up too much," they say. There is too much uncertainty. Then they ask what I think about that.

Consider this: The amount of trading volume has exploded since my early days and keeps growing. Depending on the source and the markets observed, there are realistically over one billion transactions per day valued at over $100 billion. Some days, much more.

So, who does this buying and selling? It's professionals with pedigreed résumés and the best research and information. They "vote" on the value of individual stocks every day, all day, buying and selling based on this information. Does it seem reasonable that this causes stock prices to be fair, based on the known information, just about every day?

For more background on this concept, refer to my earlier writing in this chapter or look up the Efficient Market Hypothesis by Nobel Prizing-winning professor Dr. Eugene Fama.

Or, take a practical look at historical events and compare to market movements. Would you have invested in stocks in January 1942 with the world gone crazy into World War II? In the following years, stock prices rose dramatically.

Just about every year since 1942 there has been a good reason to "wait it out in cash." Compare past headlines to results and it often makes those old headlines seem silly.

The bottom line is this: If your money is going to be needed in the next few years, or if your money is "hot" money just testing the markets, cash or shorter-term bonds are a good idea.

But based on the evidence, long-term investors—and I mean 20-year time frames here—can be rewarded with attractive gains by making a commitment to "ownership" investing to meet future financial objectives for education, retirement, gifting to charities and family, and for important personal goals.

---

alternative growth investments that can perform independent of the stock market, along with a healthy dose of fixed-maturity, fixed-interest bonds of the highest quality.

At my firm, we employ powerful portfolio monitoring tools to track the percentage held in the various asset classes and then rebalance to comply with our client's goals, as stated in her Investment Policy Statement.

Your wealth adviser should be using a similar tool or have a process for addressing your asset allocation mix regularly so you can have that "sleep-at-night portfolio."

CHAPTER SIX

Life Income at Retirement

LIFE INCOME. Have you created a plan for your future (or present) income for life that you know you cannot outlive? Do you know when you can retire and how much your income will be? Should you be saving more now for your future? Have you or your advisory team developed an estimate of the probability of success for your life-income plan?

By far the most common financial planning questions I am asked center around the need for income for life. Approaching the day when work is no longer required and every day is a Saturday is exciting but scary for many people.

The questions are similar but seek different answers:

1. When can I afford to retire?
2. How much money do I need to retire and live comfortably?
3. How much income will I have when I retire?

There are other questions, certainly, but defining the answer to the "when, how much" questions are most common.

There are a lot of books (and countless articles in the popular financial magazines) on "how to retire," and I've written one, too! That book, *The Extreme Retirement Planning Workbook*, and this chapter are based not on academic research and theoretical ideas but rather on 30 years' experience helping people make practical and sometimes difficult decisions and then observing the outcomes.

Let's start with ten reasons that you might not be able to afford retirement.

1. Retirement is apt to be for a longer period. A generation ago, a 20-year retirement was unusually long. My grandfather retired in 1963 at the standard retirement age of 65; within 20 years, both he and my grandmother had passed. Today's retirees might need to plan for a 30- or even 40-year retirement (check out your probability of living to age 90). **Longer retirements will**

A 401(k) Investment Strategy

Hopefully you have a 401(k) retirement savings plan with low-cost investment options available through your employer. This plan can be a powerful tool in your accumulation of wealth for life income after your working career.

However, some retirement savings plans have flaws, including high expenses and fees, hundreds of hard-to-select investment choices, and little in the way of helpful advice. Here's what you can do.

Rebalancing your entire portfolio, including your taxable investments, could make a lot of sense. Investing all or most of your 401(k) plan in a low-risk fixed-income fund could reduce your internal expenses, as well as place fully taxable, inefficient holdings in the tax-sheltered 401(k).

At the same time, you could increase your equity holdings in your personal, taxable account, repositioning tax-advantaged equity holdings where gains and dividend distributions could be taxed at 15 percent (or 20 percent for some taxpayers) instead of being converted to ordinary income taxable at higher rates when withdrawn from the 401(k).

Your wealth adviser should be able to help you make this transition if it is in your best interest.

(See the related sidebar on asset location in chapter 9.)

---

require more money and much more preparation.

2. Retirement is likely to be a healthier (not just longer) and more active segment of life. This suggests more opportunity for travel, more organizational and club participation, and more involvement with several generations of family. This is all great news but likely to require more money.

3. The health-care system is constantly improving and finding more ways for us to improve standards of care, longevity, and lifestyles, which cost more money. Paying for care and insurance premiums to offset these costs will be another layer of expense not considered a generation ago.

4. The "payment-for-life" pension prevalent in the past has mostly disappeared.

Beginning in the 1980s, more and more companies moved away from funding and managing pension plans and steered their employees into self-managed accounts, such as a 401(k) plan. This reduced the company's cost and responsibility for managing money and providing a guaranteed life income. Many workers today participate in some kind of voluntary contribution retirement savings plan, such as a 401(k) plan. However, it's not uncommon for them to **undercontribute and direct their investments in a manner that will not create adequate savings.**

5. Investing is more difficult. Investment returns might be lower over the next 25 or 30 years compared to the past 25 years. Lower investment returns of even 1 percent or 2 percent less would make a marked difference over a 25- or 30-year period. In the 1980s and 1990s, it was possible to lock in government bond yields that were higher than today's interest rates, but no longer. This means that it takes more of your retirement nest egg to produce presently needed cash flow, **leaving less money to be invested for growth** over the next 20 to 30 years.

6. Greater volatility of stock prices (actual and perceived) makes investing more difficult for everyone than it was a generation ago. In years past, many people were only lightly invested in stocks, or not at all. Today millions of everyday people have a large percentage of their retirement assets under their own control in a 401(k) or similar employer-sponsored retirement plan.

7. Inflation and income taxes may have a greater effect; spendable retirement income could be eroded to a greater extent over the next 30 years, and income tax rates (presently at multiyear low levels) might be increased for all income levels. **All this leaves less for the retiree to spend,** to pay basic expenses, and to support the dreamed-of lifestyle. It's possible that, while you can establish a life income stream, the purchasing power of your cash flow may decline significantly in a multidecade retirement.

8. Social Security is a concern for most Americans who intend to rely on the promised retirement income benefit. The reaction of many people is to apply for benefits at age 62, at a reduced rate (up to a 30 percent reduction), hoping to collect as much as possible. Applying for Social Security income at age 62 does offer the benefit of receiving payments up to five years earlier (for those born in 1960 and later) than normal retirement; however, in a 30-year retirement, a 30 percent discount for life is very expensive.

9. If you plan to retire before age 65, you must secure health insurance and understand its cost. Medicare is not available until age 65, **leaving most early retirees to pay the full cost of insurance**

and with less spending money to enjoy or use to pay for lifestyle expenses.

A quick list of what you should consider:

1. Save the maximum allowed in your 401(k) or other voluntary retirement or investment account ... you will need it. Most people undersave and underinvest their company retirement accounts.

2. Fund a Health Savings Account (HSA) if you are eligible and use the money accumulated for expenses in retirement.

3. Secure quality personal care insurance (i.e., long-term care insurance) as early in life as possible.

4. Determine if it is possible and advisable for you to create a *future monthly payment for life* by investing in a fixed annuity that suits your needs. A fixed-income annuity (as opposed to a deferred-savings annuity that is a money-accumulation vehicle) provides a fixed payment for life. Sometimes known as an immediate annuity, a number of "joint and survivor" options are available. The underwriting institution should be of the highest financial strength. Be sure you understand the terms, including the probable lack of return of principal that is typical of a life-payment annuity. Most retirement-planning investors should consult with an unbiased wealth adviser when making a decision regarding a life-income annuity.

5. Invest prudently and efficiently, either on your own or better yet with a top-notch financial professional.

6. Be aware of tax-efficient investing and talk with a CPA annually about income tax changes.

7. Work longer (at least consider it unless your job is a burden).

8. If possible, wait until age 70 to apply for SSI (if you are healthy and have other money you can use before then).

If you are within eight years of retiring, you are "in the zone" and should be carefully considering your resources. Meet with your wealth adviser or a retirement-income-planning professional, someone experienced in looking at projections and the income needed to live life without running out of money.

At my firm, with client input we use a wealth analysis (see the sidebar beginning on page 84) developed based on a client's individual need for income; their recommended asset mix of stocks, alternative growth investments, and bonds; and their other sources of income, including Social Security, pensions, and rental or business income.

Taking a long-term view of your assets and the ability to get payments-for-life is extremely important. Far too many investment salesmen will take a simple view that only looks at your current income and doesn't consider the impact of inflation and other expenses. And here's the thing!

Working Longer: The Value of Delaying Retirement

Age	Beginning Balance ($)	_____% Return	Annual Contribution ($)	Ending Value ($)

The Retired Ranger

I was playing a north Scottsdale, Arizona golf course a few years ago when the course "ranger," the person in charge of policing the speed of play, etc., approached our foursome. We were standing in the fairway waiting on the group in front of us; it was a perfect spring day when he pulled up in his golf car.

"How's it going?" he asked.

We replied that things were moving a little slow, but that was to be expected on a crowded golf course on a beautiful day.

Waiting with us, he made small talk, and I learned that he was from Wisconsin, the former president of a private company that had been sold to new owners, and he had moved to a vacation home that he and his wife owned in Arizona.

I said to the ranger, "This looks like a pretty good job for a retired guy. Sunny days, and I bet you play a lot of golf for free."

He agreed but didn't seem as happy or as enthusiastic as I had imagined he might be.

When I asked him about his lack of enthusiasm, he said, "Well, I'm still coming to work five or six days a week, and I still have to be here at a certain time, usually pretty early in the day. It is usually great weather and the golfers are nice, but some days when I am out here, I could just as well be back home running my company and making $500,000 a year."

The way he said it, I realized he had thought about this a lot. Although he's not a store greeter or flipping burgers, he didn't seem terribly happy. And he might as well have still been in his career where he had many specialized skills and knowledge.

I tell this story to prospective retirees, especially men, and ask, "Are you going back to work soon after you retire?"

Mistakes in retirement income planning don't always show up in the first 10 years of retirement. Unfortunately planning errors are often discovered during the second 10 years or later, when it is very difficult to recover and revise your income plan.

Bottom line: Unless you are an extremely capable planner yourself, or quite wealthy and able to afford some mistakes, you should lean on the advice of your wealth adviser and develop a projection of future income, such as the wealth analysis I noted previously.

Working Longer

If your financial resources are cutting it close and your projected life income might not exceed your expenses and spending, you need to develop a greater margin of safety. The best way to do that is to stay in the workforce longer. This will hopefully allow you to save more money, earn a few more years of investment returns on your accounts, as well as reduce the amount of income that you actually need because your retirement will be shortened by a few years. You can also earn delayed credits for your Social Security Income by waiting until age 70 to file for income benefits.

Use the "Working Longer" worksheet to take a preliminary look at how much greater your assets might be by staying on the job a few more years. This is a solution many people must consider or face running

out of money or making significant lifestyle changes.

What does "retirement downsizing" look like? Unfortunately, it can mean significant changes. Some people must sell the family home they had hoped to keep and move into a smaller home or rented apartment. Others have to quit social organizations and give up club memberships, reduce or omit charitable gifts, or cease financial assistance to family. A drastic change in lifestyle comes when the two-car family has to become the one-old-used-car family. And these aren't even worst-case scenarios.

Do You Really Want to Retire?

In my experience, many (if not most) baby boomer men are not built to retire. Women retire and tend to transition to new circumstances better than men, on average.

How many men have you known who retired, only to experience poor health or even die? In the history of the world, very few men have actually "retired." Most stopped working because they weren't physically able to continue. Until the advent of pensions and Social Security, the average guy couldn't even consider leaving work until declining health forced him to quit and rely on family for support.

Just because you're financially equipped to retire doesn't mean you're mentally and emotionally equipped. Many men just don't have enough to do to support their sense of self-worth or their reason for being after retirement. That's why a growing number of boomer men head back to work or launch new careers after retirement.

Are there any warning signs that retirement may not be for you?

To answer this question, I suggest you make a list of every imaginable planned activity you might want to pursue following retirement. Write down these ideas immediately, but keep the list open so you can add new pursuits and interests later on. Divide the list into (a) weekly post-retirement activities such as "golf on Wednesday" or "lunch with my daughter on Thursdays" and (b) nonweekly or one-time events such as "drive the Pacific Coast highway from San Diego to Seattle" or "visit all the presidential libraries." The second list is the so-called bucket list made popular in the movies.

Using the weekly list, create a planned time use worksheet (see Model Week worksheet on page 79), starting the day at the time you normally would leave home for work and concluding the day when you normally would return home from work.

This is a challenging exercise for most people. Use it as an opportunity to build confidence in your decision to retire, continue working, or launch a new career. Most people revise their lists multiple times; some delay retirement, others gain confidence in their plans and move forward into life after work. Whatever happens, give your agenda considerable thought before

leaving an enjoyable career and missing a few extra high-earning, high-accumulation final years.

I also recommend to preretirees to conduct a "feasibility study" to determine if they will enjoy retirement or go insane. Take all the vacation you have accumulated and practice retirement by staying home and doing what you intend to do, as recorded on your weekly worksheet.

Don't go out to eat every night; don't travel someplace exciting. Stay home.

Do the laundry, mow the lawn, take the garbage out, and don't think about work. Imagine that you're retired and see how well the lifestyle suits you.

At even the thought of this, many people realize they're not ready to retire. Naturally, I also sketch out what their income will look like. I discuss what income they can realistically expect from their resources and review their expenses, adjusting for reductions in expenses related to work (shirts at the laundry, parking garage) and inserting new or higher expenses associated with increased leisure time (greens fees, travel, etc.).

The retirement simulation is one of the most important services I perform for preretirees. Your wealth adviser should help you think about both the financial and nonfinancial aspects of retirement. He should also make it clear that planning is not an exact science. It's nearly impossible to forecast the future, 30 to 40 years ahead. Inflation, investment returns, medical advances,

Model Week in Retirement Worksheet

Time of Day	Monday	Tuesday	Wednesday	Thursday	Friday
7:00 to 8:00					
8:00 to 9:00					
9:00 to 10:00					
10:00 to 11:00					
11:00–12:00					
12:00 to 1:00					
1:00 to 2:00					
2:00 to 3:00					
3:00 to 4:00					
4:00 to 5:00					
5:00 to 6:00					
6:00 to 7:00					
7:00 to 8:00					
8:00 to 9:00					
9:00 to 10:00					

3 Percent Is the New 4 Percent

Conventional wisdom, in recent years, is that a retired person can withdraw 4 percent of their retirement account balance for retirement income annually and very likely never deplete their retirement nest egg. Though a good financial plan would go much deeper into the numbers, considering longevity, expected return based on risk assumption, and spending patterns, this old 4 percent rule of thumb has probably worked pretty well.

When looking back over the last several decades since the early 1980s, a typical balanced portfolio of 60 percent broadly diversified equity investments (e.g., stocks or stock mutual funds) and 40 percent fixed-income investments (bonds) has provided retired investors with income and growth. The "60-40" portfolio has produced an average annual return of over 4 percent for meaningful multiyear periods, supporting the 4 percent suggested withdrawal rate and leaving some potential for additional accumulation over time. But bond values might decline in price if interest rates rise, negatively impacting the total return of the fixed-income portion of the portfolio.

Over this last, let's call it 30 years, interest rates have mostly been trending lower. With a few stops along the way, interest rates have descended from well over 10 percent to low, low single digits. So, with that 40 percent investment in bonds, the investor captured a cash interest payment plus had some exposure to capital gains from bonds because bonds rise in value as interest rates decline.

But what about the next 30 years? Not only are interest rates low now, generating less in spendable cash, but bond values might decline in price if interest rates rise.

Stock values might also be higher, with less long-term appreciation potential than over the last 30 years. All things considered, the 4 percent distribution rate that many consider the standard for withdrawals should be reduced to 3 percent.

What is the practical impact for retirement savers? The bottom line is this: You will need quite a lot more money to support your lifestyle. Let's consider some simple math.

In the 4 percent distribution world, you would need 25 times your desired income in savings and investments. A person desiring $100,000 in portfolio income would need **$2.5 million** in capital. A 4 percent withdrawal rate on that principal would generate the needed $100,000 income.

In the 3 percent era, you would need over 33 times your desired retirement income: **$3.3 million** in capital with a 3 percent withdrawal rate produces the needed $100,000 in cash flow.

Future retirees will be faced with the need to accumulate more money by (a) saving more, (b) starting to invest sooner in life, (c) working longer, and (d) being more informed and/or better advised.

housing costs will all create variables that are unknown and unknowable.

Building a margin for safety is key to protecting you and your family from these unknowns.

Social Security

The Social Security election decision is getting more attention these days because boomer retirees are starting to understand that SSI retirement income is a marvelous resource that should be maximized.

Sadly, some people make the simplistic decision to claim income payments as soon as they are eligible, at age 62, accepting benefits that are discounted for life. They say, "I want to get as much as possible" or "I want to get some before it's all gone" before carefully considering all the facts.

However, the decision to claim retirement benefits is more involved, and life expectancy and spousal benefits must be considered. Because the retirement benefit is for life, adjusted annually for cost of living, and is fully transferrable to your surviving spouse who might collect benefits for years after you're gone, the decision is important and deserves careful consideration and calculations.

Entire books have been written on this subject and about Social Security, so I'll only address a basic consideration that wealth managers should consider immediately. The Social Security Administration website is a good place to start if you want to do your own initial research: www.ssa.gov.

For those who are affluent, healthy, and confident of their longevity, the smartest approach to Social Security is, in my view, to delay claiming until age 70. For today's retiree, benefits are increased for life by ⅔ percent per month for each month income is delayed between full retirement age (age 66 for individuals born between 1943 and 1954) and age 70. The 48-month delay represents an increase in the monthly SSI retirement payment of 32 percent over your life and the life of your surviving spouse!

(If you were born in 1960 or later, you are eligible for your full benefit or FRA at age 67. Since you can only earn delayed credits of 2/3 percent per month for 36 months, your maximum is 124 percent if you wait to claim until age 70. Still, this might be a significant amount to you or your spouse during a long retirement.)

Though much more thought should be done and more thorough projections should be made, the break-even point for delaying benefits or collecting at full retirement age is considering whether you or your spouse will live another 17 years (to age 83, approximately).

My firm uses a detailed program to consider all factors, including anticipated life expectancy, when advising our clients on the best claiming decision. Because the life income from Social Security Retirement is substantial, you should too.

If you are many years from retirement, you should develop projections of what your financial resources could accumulate to at your envisioned retirement date.

To increase your income for life resources, step up your wealth accumulation efforts in your tax-advantaged retirement accounts. Learn the history of stock market returns and maximize your exposure to long-term growth while being mindful of your comfort with financial volatility and uncertainty.

Common mistakes:

Undercontributing, especially early in life, and not harnessing the power of compounding is a common mistake. The money accumulated before age 30 is extremely important and will grow into a large percentage of the pool of money that you eventually accumulate.

Maximize your contributions to your voluntary company retirement savings plan, such as a 401(k). Many people make the mistake of only contributing the "matched" portion.

Underinvesting, by leaving contributions too conservatively invested for long periods of time, is another common mistake. It's not at all uncommon for me to review the retirement plans of people with many years to work and find large chunks of money invested in the cash or low-yielding investment options.

Consider the following very dramatic example:

Saver #1 earns $100,000 per year and contributes 3 percent of his wages to his company plan, capturing the company match for total contributions of $6,000 per year. He hates volatility and decides to take the conservative approach, leaving his money invested for 30 years in short-term, liquid, and lower-yielding investments that average a 2 percent return.

Saver #2 also earns $100,000 per year but contributes $17,000 per year and gets the company match of $3,000 for a total of $20,000. She realizes that she has 30 years before she needs the money and leaves it invested in a broadly diversified growth account and averages an 8 percent return over the years.

How much more does Saver #2 have after 30 years?

First consider this: Saver #1 contributed $90,000 of his own money and collected $90,000 in matched contributions from his employer, for a total of $180,000 saved over this 30-year period.

Saver #2 contributed $510,000 of her money plus the additional $90,000 in matched contribution from the employer, for a total of $600,000. This is an additional $420,000 for Saver #2.

For impact, imagine the actual difference in applying 2 percent return to the annual savings of Saver #1 and 8 percent investment gains to the annual contributions of Saver #2. In this example, Saver #1 accumulates $248,276. Saver #2 has a retirement portfolio of $2,446,917. Though Saver #2 set aside $420,000 more in her account, over 30 years the total difference is a stunning $2,198,641. (Please note: Though we believe this example to be reasonable, these projections are for illustration purposes only and are not meant to reflect actual or guaranteed results.)

Saving in retirement accounts is the workhorse of most Americans. Why?

1. It harnesses compounding at equity/ growth rates of return over what can be a potentially long period of time.
2. The contribution can avoid income taxation in the year it is earned and deposited to the plan, reducing current taxation during higher-income-earning years.
3. The principal and all of the gains are shielded from taxes until withdrawn in retirement.
4. Many employers match some percentage of the plan participant's earnings.

Determining the amount of money you need to live comfortably for the rest of your life will take significant planning and insights about how you want your life to look in retirement. After completing this planning is an excellent time to turn your

The Question Most Asked

My life has been centered on my work as a financial adviser. And I live in a modest-sized Midwestern town—Lincoln, Nebraska—so it's not uncommon that I meet people socially who know of me and the work I've been doing. It's all part of living in a community.

After a handshake and small talk, it's not at all uncommon for my new friend to ask financial questions, and I love talking about saving, investing, and planning, so I do nothing to discourage it.

You might have already guessed what people ask about. It's the "when" and "how much" questions that surround retirement and leaving the workforce for a life where every day is a Saturday. The questions usually start fairly general, something like: "What are people doing to retire these days?" And eventually, the questions progress to something more specific and personal: "How would I know when I have enough money to quit working for life?"

In addition to reading this chapter, you might consider engaging a financial planning professional who uses powerful planning tools to help you chart (and annually rechart) your course from the present to your future retirement.

Any serious planning firm will have technology-driven tools that lend clarity to what could be an otherwise murky financial future. These software packages must mix in a number of variables, such as

- What resources do you have at this point in time?
- How much can you add annually?
- Do you have pension income that will support retirement?
- What will your SSI be and when should you claim it?
- What rate of return is reasonable, based on your ability, need, and willingness to take investment risk, and given investing's uncertainty?
- How much money do you anticipate you will need, after taxes?
- What will the inflation rate be, and can you factor that into your future need for income?

My colleagues and I, for example, engage a proprietary Monte Carlo simulation-based tool we simply refer to as a wealth analysis. Factoring in all the data listed above, this program develops our best estimate of a client's potential success with a confidence factor that goes up to 100 percent.

"How much is enough?" is fine for small talk at a social event. But when it comes to your real-life financial success, take time to connect with a financial professional who can help you gather the necessary input of data, will help you assess your need to accept risk, and will stand ready to update your plan regularly.

Unless you know the answer to your "retirement" questions, you cannot become financially confident.

The Wealth Analysis

The wealth analysis is a comprehensive tool that incorporates a number of factors, some definite dollar needs and amounts and projections of future income. This powerful tool then develops an estimate of a client's probability of life-income success. You or your financial team should develop and update a "feasibility study" such as this as often as annually.

These Monte Carlo simulations are based on thousands of assumptions involving your time horizon, your investment assets available, your asset mix of stock and bonds, your pension and Social Security payments, inflation rates, and your anticipated withdrawals. Studying the results of these illustrations can be helpful in setting your asset allocation policy, determining your need to save more for retirement, and understanding what amount of money you can anticipate living on in the future.

attention to what will happen to the assets and cash in your possession when you die, also known as estate planning, the topic of the next chapter on residual wealth.

CHAPTER SEVEN

Residual Wealth: What Happens to the Money You Don't Need?

RESIDUAL WEALTH. Who or what will get your money when your time on planet Earth is over? Do you want to transfer money during your life or at life's end? Will children and other heirs get your unconsumed wealth or will it go to charities?

If you have accumulated wealth, you should consider what happens to your money if you depart Earth. Sorry, it happens. To everybody. So think about it.

Wealth advisers are generally not experts at estate planning and not licensed to create legal documents. But they should be knowledgeable and aware of issues that might arise so they can urge you or any client to get valuable legal advice when needed.

First, we should answer the question, what is residual wealth?

Residual wealth is the money or assets left over at the end of life, or the assets that you will not need to live comfortably during your lifetime. It's your extra money. This is the money that should be identified as early

as possible so thoughtful, intentional plans can be laid out based on your wishes.

I prefer the term *residual wealth* to the more common *estate planning* because, among other things, it isn't necessary to wait until death to distribute some of your wealth to heirs and worthy causes, assuming you won't need the money during your lifetime.

Most Americans fall into one of three categories, the result of which dictates how they should approach residual wealth planning.

Planner's Perspective: Though residual wealth planning is very important, it is usually not seen as urgent and sometimes not seriously approached until too late (or almost too late), and many smart alternatives and opportunities are never seriously evaluated. Of all the financial planning that real people can do, wealth transfers, along with the strategic purchase of life insurance, is frequently delayed or ignored completely.

The Irrevocable Life Insurance Trust (ILIT)

The ILIT (pronounced *eye-lit*) is a financial strategy that can help transfer significant wealth to heirs while avoiding income and estate taxes. If you are (or become) wealthy, highly taxed, and you wish to transfer significant sums to your heirs as beneficiaries, this section could be valuable to you.

By combining the best traits of a life insurance contract, the tax efficiency of the irrevocable trust, and the desire to share wealth with heirs/beneficiaries/survivors, the ILIT can multiply family wealth significantly.

Here's how it works:

First, the death benefit payment of a life insurance policy is normally income-tax-free, even though the premiums paid are less than the death benefit payment. So, to be clear, the "gain" on a policy that pays at your death is income-tax-free.

Generally, assets under your control when you die are includable in your taxable estate. If you're in a financial situation where you are over certain asset thresholds (as of this writing, generally over $11.2 million per person), your assets over this amount can be taxed as much as 40 percent as of 2018. The proceeds of a life insurance policy you own at your death will probably be included in your estate for tax purposes.

However, assets in a trust that cannot be changed by you (called irrevocable) are generally not included in your estate as long as certain conditions are met. Therefore, with the help of your estate-planning lawyer, you create an irrevocable trust designed to own insurance on your life. The proceeds of that life insurance policy—payable to the trust, which pays the death benefit payment to your heirs—are not included in your estate.

Drafted properly and funded with gifts or cash transfers that meet specific criteria (called a Crummey provision, named for a landmark court case), the payment from the life insurance benefit through the ILIT can be income-tax-free *and* estate-tax-free.

Consider the rate of return you would have to earn on a taxable investment to equal the income tax-free and estate tax-free return of the ILIT result.

In addition to the favorable tax treatment, transferring wealth to heirs with life insurance proceeds is effortless for the recipients. There are no auctions, no sales of property, no valuations, and the transfer is not generally subject to probate.

If you are in a high income tax bracket due to your earnings, you have accumulated assets that exceed the excluded amount for estate taxes, you have heirs who you wish to benefit from your wealth generation, and you are insurable, take the time to discuss the ILIT with your wealth-transfer-planning team, which could include your estate-planning attorney, your life insurance professional, and your wealth adviser.

The first category is composed of Americans who have assets or wealth totaling something less than the amount that they really need to live comfortably for life. This category is the largest of the three groups by a large margin. They will leave little or nothing at all to heirs. You might be in this category now but will grow out of it, so pay attention to your wealth and monitor your net worth as discussed earlier in this book.

A number of the people in this Wealth Distribution Group #1 have little or no money and live on dribbles of income from small pensions, disability payments, Social Security, and the kindness of charities and relatives. Others in this group have some resources but find it necessary to reduce their standard of living in retirement to not run out of money. Though they need to tend to wills and financial and health-care directives, there is little need to plan for the involved transfer of wealth because there is none.

Wealth Distribution Group #2 is those people who can be fairly sure they have enough money and retirement income resources to live the rest of their lives and probably leave something to their heirs and favorite charities, but not so much that there will be much, if any, federal estate taxes payable at their passing.

Most of the people in this category have investment advisers and some sort of financial plan in place and are the "bread-and-butter" clients of the typical investment or wealth management firm. These people usually have wills, trusts, and other planning documents in place, though they are often not updated or reconsidered on a regular basis.

Make sure your documents are up-to-date and review them at least every couple years or anytime you have a change of any importance (new wealth, new heirs, etc.).

The smallest category is Wealth Distribution Group #3, the wealthiest Americans who have substantial resources, money in the bank, investments, real estate, businesses, and probably significant life insurance benefits that will be payable to heirs. These people have more money than they need to live the rest of their lives. This group should seek highly capable estate planners and undergo an annual review of every facet of their wealth-transfer planning during their lifetimes—or at least consider their situations and how circumstances may have changed every few years.

Which category describes your situation?

Based on your assessment of your circumstances, refer to the section that applies to you and follow the action plan provided.

Group #1 Action Plan

Though your assets and financial resources may be modest or nonexistent, you should seek out an attorney, perhaps legal aid or a lawyer offering "pro bono" services to people who cannot afford a lawyer, and review your situation. You may be able to direct most of your assets to loved ones who survive you by creating joint accounts and using beneficiary designations, but some assets must be transferred by a will. Additionally, you should seek help in drafting a power of attorney for health care so that your wishes may be carried out if you are unable to speak for yourself.

If you die "intestate" (without a valid will), your state has a plan for the distribution of your property that is unlikely to be in line with your wishes.

Also, in the absence of direction from your will, minor children will be entrusted to whomever your state decides.

Bottom line: Sit down with a lawyer and create a will and other important documents. You may not need to change these instruments for years (although you might if your assets and wealth grow).

Group #2 Action Plan

You almost certainly have a will and maybe a revocable living trust. Hopefully your documents have been updated in the last year or two, or the last time you had a life or family event that changed your situation.

My suggestion for you is to get your will and estate planning documents out and read them. Map out where the assets will go

The Basics of Wills and Estate Planning: When I Die

During planning sessions in which wills and estate are discussed, some people will say, "If something happens to me..." and then trail off. What they should really be saying is **"When I die"** because we will all pass on. To make things easier for the people we love, we should all engage in lifetime and end-of-life asset transfer planning.

First, at the very least, you should have a will. If you don't have one at all, you should get one. Find a lawyer skilled in this practice area (your wealth adviser can help you) and schedule an appointment. Review the beneficiary designations on your IRAs, company retirement accounts, life insurance policies, annuities, trust documents, and "pay-on-death" or "transfer-on-deeath" accounts with a financial institution—anything with a beneficiary—to ensure that the designations still match your wishes. When meeting with new clients, it's not uncommon to discover they need to change beneficiaries from ex-spouses, former business partners, and deceased individuals to more appropriate (living!) family members.

At the same time, review your joint accounts to ensure these are also to your liking. Joint accounts become the sole property of the other owner when you die. If you have an account or accounts joint with one of your children, but you want multiple children to share in the property, you may have a problem.

Wealth distribution planning is important but usually not urgent and doesn't get the proper attention. Take action. Get help and advice from qualified professionals.

---

when you die. Is your residual wealth distribution in line with your wishes?

You probably have charitable intent you are meeting now with modest "checkbook charity," but in limited amounts because you're not sure how much you will need to live the rest of your life. It might be tax wise to consider making a charity the primary beneficiary on part of your retirement plan assets so that the assets are available to you during your life but pass to the charity at your death.

Selecting the Right Attorney

To choose a good attorney to assist you with your transfer planning, follow the same rules you'd follow when looking for any other adviser. Don't assume that the nice lawyer at your service club, church, or golf club is the right one (though he or she might be). It's nice to work with somebody you like, but for this important work you need to seek the best counsel and advice.

Most wealth advisers can recommend a good attorney (preferably several, so you can choose) from the area who specializes in this type of professional work. When I'm working with clients outside of my home territory, I often visit the website of the American College of Trust and Estate Counsel, an invitation-only organization of estate planning lawyers who specialize in wealth-transfer planning.

At a minimum, you should expect your wealth adviser to give you proactive advice and make you aware of issues that might impact you. Your wealth adviser might even take charge and organize a meeting of your other advisers, including your attorney, your life insurance professional, and your tax professional to discuss your present plan and make recommendations.

Group #3 Action Plan

You have substantial resources and the chances are pretty good your estate or family will pay estate taxes when you have passed on. Just because you don't like it or you don't think it's fair are not valid reasons that you should avoid revisiting your plan on a regular, probably annual basis. Failure to plan and update plans can be expensive and is likely to leave your lifetime accumulation of assets distributed in a manner that might be contrary to your wishes.

How much do you want to bequeath to your heirs and beneficiaries—now and after you die?

Consider how old your beneficiaries will be if you wait until you die to transfer some of your wealth: 55, 65, 70, or even older? Do you really want to wait to transfer wealth to your children when they have already reached retirement? Why not arrange to make lifetime gifts—not just to children

Balancing Inheritances

A common problem for wealthy business and property owners who wish to transfer their wealth to heirs is "making it all even." Often, a son or daughter is involved in the family business (or farm or ranch, etc.), and he or she will continue operating the business after the founders pass away. For many reasons, it's awkward or difficult to manage a business that's jointly owned by siblings who are not active in the enterprise. A great solution is to pass the entire business to the child/children/heirs who have been working in it, leaving the other heirs an equalizing amount from life insurance benefits, paid in cash at the death of the original business owner.

Your wealth-transfer-planning team can help you create a plan that "keeps the business in the family" as well as "keeps the family together" by keeping inherited assets separate.

and grandchildren but also to favorite charities and other worthy causes that you support—and watch how people and organizations you love benefit from your generosity.

Because you have wealth beyond what you are likely to need to live the rest of your life, you are in a great position to make gifts during your lifetime to your future heirs and to charities that you want to benefit from your life's work. While other people are limited in how generous they can be to heirs and charities, you can actually see your distributed wealth at work (as well as get credit and enjoy some level of respect during your lifetime). Based on my observation of people over my 30-plus years of experience, lifetime giving (as opposed to end-of-life-only giving) is far more valuable to both the receiver and giver.

You may be able to arrange your tax matters in a way to decrease the amount of estate tax that will be payable at your death. And, you may have to rearrange your affairs again and again as tax code changes are made from time to time.

Your wealth transition planning team should never be disbanded. Make sure that your wealth advisers, your estate planning attorney, your CPA or other tax professional, and your life insurance professional are all working together to deliver the best

Important Contacts

Carefully consider the most important "first calls" your family will need to make if some morning you don't wake up. Burdened by the grief and sadness that surrounds the passing of a loved one, many survivors have to try to figure out the next steps to take. You can make that much easier by completing the following "Trusted Adviser Worksheet" I have created. Go ahead and make a copy, with my permission.

Important Contacts and Phone Numbers

Funeral Arrangements Were Made By _____

Lawyer: Last Will and Trusts _____

Trusted Life Insurance Professional _____

Wealth Adviser _____

possible advice and action regarding your distribution of wealth.

At least annually, and more often if you have a change in family circumstances or in your financial situation, you should carefully rethink your wealth distribution plan. This will very likely require that you spend some time in the office of your estate planning lawyer, who will probably bill you for the time and advice. Just get used to it because it's worth it for you. Improper planning and unintended distributions can be expensive and disruptive to your family.

My last word on this often-neglected subject: You need a plan! If you haven't gotten to it yet, you're not alone. Not long ago I met with a successful lawyer and his wife. When I went through the Eight Points with them, I discovered ... guess what? They had no wills at that time. But they do now.

Make this important planning a priority if you have people you love and who love you.

As you decide on the transfer of wealth to your heirs and charities, consider how you can transfer assets as well as know-how during your lifetime, and after, to people or institutions you love and view as valuable to the world, the topic of chapter 8.

Recommended additional reading: *Strangers in Paradise: How Families Adapt to Wealth across Generations* by James Grubman, PhD, and *Preparing Heirs: Five Steps to a Successful Transition of Family Wealth and Values* by Roy Williams and Vic Preisser.

CHAPTER EIGHT

Improving Someone's Life with Education and Life Skills

EDUCATION FUNDING. Do you know a young person (or anyone) you would like to assist in paying for college or other vocational education? Are you using tax-efficient methods of accumulation to set this money aside? How much will you need to educate these fortunate people? Can you make a difference by leaving a legacy of knowledge by mentoring someone?

If your college years are not a distant memory, you know that higher education is expensive (as are private high schools) but can be worth many multiples of the cost for students that learn and apply the life skills these institutions teach. If you have a child, grandchild, or other relative who has a need for an education, you can make a difference in the life of this prospective student and have a positive impact on the world by supporting their achievement (i.e., paying tuition, living expenses, etc.).

What does college cost? The range is approximately $20,000 per year for room, board, tuition, fees, etc., at a state university or college and up to over $40,000 for many private colleges. Elite national universities can be double this amount, and who knows where these costs will go over the next 10 to 15 years. It's anybody's guess but a good bet that the costs are going to rise.

Before we talk about paying for college, let's consider whether college is a requirement for every person. Based on conversations with my clients and their families, I've come to realize that far too many parents believe a college education is a must—that no matter what their child's talents, goals, and interests, he or she absolutely has to go to college in pursuit of a bachelor's degree.

I know a young man, pressured by his parents to attend college, who drifted through a few years of it and didn't do well, then ended up leaving without a degree. However, with a little technical instruction, he flourished when he got into the workforce and is a whiz with electronics, computers, and putting things together. Though he matured as a person during his four years of college "attendance," he could have learned more suitable and

What's More Valuable ... the Money or the Method of Earning It?

Many families agonize over the right wealth distribution plan, and it's understandable. Transferring wealth earned during your lifetime should be done only after very careful consideration and planning.

Still, many, if not most, benefactors fail to consider the most valuable transfer of all ... the knowledge and mindset that it took to create the wealth or assets transferred.

For example, which is more valuable: An elite golfer's money or his golf swing at the height of his career? Or, which is worth more: a Grammy recording artist's massive wealth or his ability to write music and perform for decades?

Think about your assets, your wealth, and your abilities and knowledge. Which legacy could potentially be more valuable to your heirs? Your assets and money or your ability to build a company, save and accumulate money, or achieve success in the corporate or business world?

Determine a way to convey or teach your natural or self-learned skills; they'll become a very valuable legacy to your heirs. Hire someone to interview you and to write your story and/or record your spoken history of success and the foundation of your legacy. Your heirs and family members will capture the valuable story of your success and skills.

---

usable information with a less expensive and time-consuming education, all while enjoying his work and on-the-job education.

You can probably think of someone just like this young man.

Where applicable, part of the financial planning process should be educating yourself about educational opportunities and being sure you and your student understand them, and then evaluating his or her interests and life goals.

In general, attending a prestigious private university is a valuable experience, but more valuable for some students than others. For example, attending an Ivy League college or national university offers a great education and perhaps an even better opportunity for networking and making future business and social connections with highly successful people who are part of your college network. If your son or daughter wants to be a Wall Street investment banker, attending an elite university will probably establish contacts with more future colleagues and clients than some financial types meet in an entire working career.

To sum it up, determine if your children's education will really help them realize life and career goals or merely give them a free "fun ride" for four or five years while they grow up a little more. If it's the latter, are you prepared to support them if they discover that they can't earn a decent living?

Consider this: Plumbers can earn more than English teachers. I'm not suggesting that one vocation is better than another, but don't make the mistake of equating every college education with higher earning potential. It's just not the case. Understand that if your child wants to attend an Ivy League college and become an English teacher, the costs of that education might not end for you at graduation. You may have to supply financial support for many years after graduation while your child struggles to earn a living wage. Realizing this, a small liberal arts college or teachers college might be the right choice.

Paying for College Costs

Many parents (and grandparents) have a strong desire to pay for their children's entire college experience. From my perspective, sometimes that is a great idea and wonderful gift, but in other cases it doesn't work out so well to give the student a free four years with no requirement to succeed and no firmly established goal.

So here are some educational motivating arrangements that I have seen in action, for your consideration:

One of my clients, a man I'll call Rob, wanted to support his children's decisions. And he did. But not like you might think.

When each of his three children went to college, he helped them with some spending money but required that they borrow their tuition, their living expenses at the dormitories, and their books and lab fees. He promised to pay off the loans the day they graduated with a bachelor's degree.

The result? This man's youngsters went to college, had some fun, and managed to graduate with their intended degrees in four years, a feat in this era of five-year undergraduate degrees, with solid grades and offers for employment before graduation. He wrote a check for the total loan payoff when each of them graduated.

Others that I have observed participate by paying a percentage, saying, "You pay half, and I'll pay half." Though not in the majority, some families expect each child to make it on their own with only a modest

The 529 College Savings Plan

The 529 College Savings Plan is one of the most powerful savings tools for future educational expenses. Legally known as "Qualified Tuition Plans," they are usually referred to as the 529 plan after that section of the Internal Revenue Code.

Here are the basics:

- The plans are sponsored by states, state agencies, and educational institutions. Each state has its own rules regarding contributions and deductibility. It's important to understand the advantages of the offering of your state.
- Earnings on the contributions used for qualified educational expenses are federally income-tax-free.
- Some states allow a *state income tax deduction* for contributions.
- Most plans have high contribution limits and are available to anyone, not limited by income thresholds, and can be an excellent gifting and estate-planning tool.
- Beneficiaries can be changed to another qualified family member at any time.
- Starting with the 2018 tax year, you can use money saved in a 529 plan to pay for private school tuition for K–12. Be sure to check if your state has agreed to the federal change.

Your wealth adviser can be a valuable resource in making a decision on which plan to use, how much to contribute, and how to allocate the investments within the plan.

---

amount of support from parents or other family members.

Still others pay the full cost but only as long as a high grade point average is achieved and maintained.

Sadly, I've witnessed thousands, probably millions, of client dollars spent on higher education for children who were meandering though college with no clear goal. You can probably think of a few less-than-zealous students on a free four-year ride.

My own college expenses were paid for my first two years with a so-called "full-ride" basketball scholarship at a two-year junior college. I got straight C grades.

Then, I finished my last two years at my alma mater and had to work nights while going to school to pay the tuition and my living costs; I made the Dean's List!

Before funding college, discuss your expectations with your prospective college student.

Today there are a number of ways to save for college, including accounts sponsored by each state. Though each state has its own version with different limits, investments, and state income tax deductibility, these 529 plans generally share a few common traits.

First, the contributions can be deductible for state income tax purposes (depending on the plan and state). Next, the money invested grows without current taxation on the dividends, interest, and growth. Then, if used for bona fide college expenses as defined by the plan when withdrawn, the money withdrawn is federally income-tax-free.

Your wealth adviser can give you more detail on the various college funding plans available, as well as other education funding options.

There are other choices you can make if you decide to support higher education but do not have a specific student you desire to support or assist. You can make contributions directly to colleges or their foundations, as well as to organizations that can facilitate education for worthy students. These transfers can be made during your lifetime as a gift or at the end of your life by bequest.

For many families, educational expenses are a substantial expenditure that affects the lifestyle of the family during the college years and in many cases for life, reducing resources for other pursuits or retirement. But one other category of expenses is likely to be greater than educational costs... taxes, the topic of the final point in the chapter ahead.

CHAPTER NINE

Taxes: Your Largest Overhead Expense

TAX-WISE PLANNING. What percentage of your total income goes to pay income tax? What percentage of your net worth do you pay in income tax? Do you meet with your tax professional annually (preferably in the late fall) to consider tax-wise opportunities? Will your estate be subject to federal estate taxes or state inheritance taxes? If so, are you using tax-advantaged methods of transferring wealth? Are your investment assets positioned in a way to take advantage of the current income tax laws?

For many working Americans who are saving and investing, the taxes they pay annually are probably more than their mortgage payments, more than cost of living, and more than any other expense category. Perhaps more important, the amounts paid annually for federal and state income taxes are usually far greater than the amounts working people can save for their future and for the futures of the people they love.

As your income grows, working with a tax professional is strongly recommended if you have high tax bills, rising taxable income, and complex matters to consider. Your wealth adviser may not be licensed or trained to give detailed advice on these matters, but he should be able to effectively identify areas where you can make adjustments, take advantage of income-tax-reducing accounts, and, in general, help you consider how you can minimize or avoid taxes.

So, just to be clear, you should schedule a meeting with your tax professional during the "nontax season," which is basically between October 15 and the end of the calendar year. The fact that you might have to pay extra fees to your tax advisers should not be a reason to avoid this meeting and valuable advice. This review will help you by identifying specific actions you can take to reduce or minimize the amount of tax you pay.

On an ongoing basis, your wealth adviser should proactively help you in the following areas:

1. When managing your taxable investments, the impact of sales and repositioning should be considered.

Traditional IRA versus the Roth IRA

Created under the Employee Retirement Income Security Act of 1974, the traditional Individual Retirement Account (IRA) allows contributions to be made "pretax," as they are deducted from income on the account holder's income tax return. In other words, a $5,000 contribution would only cost $3,000 in current cash flow for someone in a 40 percent combined income tax bracket.

The deposit to the account grows based on the assets in the account, such as a stock mutual fund, with no current taxation. This allows the entire original contribution plus the investment returns to be compounded without income tax payments until money is withdrawn at retirement.

The Roth IRA works differently. The contribution to the account is *not* deductible, and it grows without taxation in the same way as the traditional IRA. But here's the difference: The original principal deposit and all subsequent returns are withdrawn tax-free at retirement!

Before you get too excited about the Roth, understand that the net after-tax results are the exact same for both accounts if tax rates and investment returns are identical.

So, which is better for you? If you are in a lower tax bracket now but anticipate being in a higher tax situation when you withdraw from your IRA during retirement, then the Roth is the best choice for you. Generally, younger investors, in a lower tax bracket and with years to invest for high growth, are better off with the Roth IRA.

If you are in a maximum tax bracket now with the possibility of a lower tax rate later, then the traditional IRA is probably better for you. Also, if you are nearer retirement and investing more conservatively, with lower expected returns, the deduction for the traditional contribution could be more valuable to you than the tax-free withdrawal in a few years.

The same decision-making process can apply to the deductible "pretax" 401(k) contribution and the "after-tax" 401(k) contribution.

Experience has taught me that avoiding taxes by itself is never a good reason to not take action. I remember the client who would not sell inherited stock that had soared from a few thousand dollars in value to nearly $1 million in the late 1990s (also known as the "dot-com" era). Wanting to avoid capital gains taxes, he would not sell a grossly overvalued stock, and, you might have guessed it, the stock eventually plummeted back to its original price levels.

2. Tax-advantaged investments in municipal bonds can be especially attractive if you have substantial taxable interest income. The interest earned on "tax-free bonds" can be both state and federal income-tax-free and at times can offer extremely competitive taxable equivalent returns, though not without risks. Municipal bonds are subject to availability and change in price. They are subject to market risk and interest rate fluctuations if sold prior to maturity. Bond values will decline as interest rates rise. Interest income may be subject to the alternative minimum tax. Municipal bonds are federally tax-free, but other state and local taxes may apply. If sold prior to maturity, capital gains tax could apply.

3. The workhorse for most working individuals is the tax-deferred retirement savings account, such as a 401(k) or, for many, the Individual Retirement Account (IRA), which offers a reduction of current income taxes via an income tax deduction or reduction of taxable income and can also delay the tax on the earnings in the retirement account as a result of the tax deferral feature. Money deposited into one of these accounts (there are many varieties, and your wealth adviser can explain them to you) can lower your tax bill this year as well as provide investment choices that can grow without taxation to be used in retirement and possibly passed on to heirs.

4. Though Roth IRAs and after-tax 401(k) accounts do not offer a current year reduction of tax, the growing assets are not subject to income taxes as they accumulate and they are not generally taxable when withdrawn for retirement. Depending on your current and future anticipated income tax situation, forgoing the current deduction in favor of fully tax-free withdrawals in the future may be the best route for you. Your wealth adviser should be a valuable source of information and advice in this area.

5. There are other tax-advantaged investments that offer incentives in the form of reduced taxes. Please take care to fully understand these investments and get a second opinion from a tax professional. Often these programs can offer a good tax reduction but fail to make money, so what's the point? I'd rather

Havesting Losses

It may sound silly to talk about "harvesting" losses, but there really is value in proactively reviewing holdings in search of capital losses that can be realized and used to offset capital gains, current ordinary income, or carried into the future to be used to offset future taxable income.

At the very least, harvesting losses delays paying tax in the current year.

At the same time, cash from the sale of the losing position is reinvested in a new holding, possibly reestablishing a lower cost basis in a stronger performing investment or instituting a new, more appropriate investment.

Why not delay taxes and upgrade holdings, especially if transaction costs are low?

For investors who hold a handful of individual common stocks in an advisory account, this process is fairly simple and is often done toward the end of the year.

However, for diversified portfolios of mutual funds, with quarterly reinvestment of dividends or capital gains, the number of purchases can be hard to proactively identify. Also, year-end might not be the optimum time to take advantage of "swaps" (the simultaneous sale of a losing position and investment in a new, upgraded holding), as they can surface throughout the calendar year.

Powerful software can assist your wealth advisory team in proactively discovering opportunities to consider for tax-loss harvesting and repositioning throughout the year.

---

you made money and paid income taxes on the gains without undue risks. (I remember a client that once held $1 million in his noninterest-earning checking account and refused to transfer some of the cash to an interest-bearing account because it would increase his income tax!)

6. Annuities offer the ability to defer gains and earnings and come in many different forms. Some annuities are appropriate for long-term growth and

tax deferral, while others are designed to provide stability of principal or life income. Any annuity contract should be considered a long-term investment that should be very carefully evaluated before purchase.

7. In managing an entire portfolio, special attention should be paid to "asset location," where tax-advantaged holdings are placed in personal, taxable accounts and tax-inefficient investments are held in tax-sheltered retirement plans. (See the sidebar on this important topic on page 108.)

The points above address only income taxes. For financially successful people, estate taxes could be greater than the income taxes they pay over a lifetime. Though I am not going to cover estate taxes further, consider this: After earning money, paying income taxes on the earnings, saving and investing the money, and paying taxes on dividends, interest, and capital gains, up to 40 percent of an estate over $11.2 million can be owed in federal estate taxes. This does not include state inheritance taxes levied by some states.

As discussed in chapter 7, planning for the orderly distribution of assets accumulated during life and at the end of life to heirs and charities is an extremely important undertaking that should be a priority, especially as your assets grow.

So, now that we've covered the last of the Eight Points, it's time to consider the big

picture and discover the calm that comes from Financial Confidence, knowing where you want to go, having an idea of how you will get there, and understanding how you will track progress, reduce risks and current taxes, increase returns, and what your income will (or could) look like in the future.

Asset Location

Buckingham Strategic Wealth was founded in 1994 by two practicing CPAs who felt there was a better way to invest than just buying and selling stocks through a stockbroker. They hoped that if they took care of their clients, in three to five years they would be advising clients with a total of $100 million in their care.

Well, their "client-first" approach worked, and now the firm and its associated firms manage over $30 billion for thousands of families.

Using tax-wise strategies is part of the client-first DNA of Buckingham, and I'll share an approach that I believe is especially valuable and that you should be looking for from your wealth advisory team.

The concept of "asset location" is extremely important and often overlooked by even top financial people.

Stocks and stock mutual funds pay dividends and realize long-term capital gains, over time, and are taxed at advantageous rates of 15 percent (or potentially 20 percent, depending on your income). This is often less than half of the maximum tax rates.

Fixed-income bonds and CDs are highly tax inefficient and fully taxable as they are earned as ordinary income.

Often, we find that investors have a mix of these two broad classes in their taxable accounts, as well as in their tax-sheltered retirement accounts (e.g., 401(k) plans and IRAs). Can you see why this can be a tax-inefficient mistake?

Wouldn't it be best to hold all (or most) of your equity investments with the tax-advantaged dividends and long-term capital gains in a personal/ taxable account? Holding equities in a retirement account does defer the tax on dividends and gains, but it converts lower-taxed dividends and long-term gains to fully taxable earnings in the future when withdrawn from the plan.

Placing stock mutual funds in a personal account also offers the opportunity to do some "tax-swapping" to reduce income taxes during periods of decline. Losses within an IRA are not deductible for tax purposes.

Additionally, long-held equity assets that grow significantly are eligible for a "step-up" in cost basis when the account owner passes. The otherwise taxable gain can disappear with the estate step-up in value. No such step-up is available within an IRA or other retirement account.

Where it is consistent with your overall risk tolerance and asset mix, it makes sense for most of us to hold equity mutual funds and stocks in our taxable account and to fill our retirement account with appropriate fixed income or other tax-inefficient investments.

CHAPTER TEN

Putting It All Together

I'm told that many people buy books and never read past the first few pages, and most fail to finish a "how-to" book like this. Hopefully you've been able to find enough valuable insights to read the parts of the text that apply most significantly to you, if not the entire book.

In wrapping up all the concepts, the following questions are designed to help you consider what areas of your life and wealth you have mastered and maybe pinpoint a few areas that need some attention and improvement.

On this and the following page, or on a separate sheet of paper, write down your answers, thoughts, and actions to take below each of the Eight Points. An experienced wealth adviser can help you as you consider each of these areas; however, my suggestion is that you carefully contemplate your thoughts prior to meeting your advisers. Knowing what you want to achieve and where you stand without any outside influence is likely to yield the best results for you and the people you love.

1. Do you have clarity on what you really want to have happen in your life? Can you envision at least one pursuit that could keep you happily occupied for the rest of your life?

   _____

   _____

   _____

   _____

2. Do you or your advisers have a way to monitor your progress? What are you doing to analyze your portfolio's results and your entire financial net worth?

   _____

   _____

   _____

   _____

3. Are the financial risks you cannot afford to bear offset with insurance or other "assets" in place if you need cash?

_____

_____

_____

_____

4. Is your wealth accumulation and management plan repeatable and based on historical evidence?

_____

_____

_____

_____

5. Are you confident you can quit working (someday) and have an income for life?

_____

_____

_____

_____

6. If you have any "residual wealth" you're not going to use or spend during your lifetime, do you know where it will go when you are gone?

_____

_____

_____

_____

7. Who do you want to help educate by providing financial assistance? Is there some legacy besides money you can pass on as part of your wealth-transfer planning?

_____

_____

_____

_____

8. Are you tax efficient? What percentage of your income is paid in taxes: federal income tax, state income tax, local income tax, and property taxes?

_____

_____

_____

_____

Who is the adviser that you can trust and depend on to help you complete the answers to these questions? The wealth adviser is the one adviser in the best position to be your "financial quarterback." Why? Because he's aware of your entire situation in more detail than your attorney, tax professionals, insurance agents, and other investment salespeople. Your wealth adviser should be in contact with you more often than your tax, legal, and insurance advisers and has more opportunity to know your needs and your situation. He should be able to help you bring all of these areas of your life together, proactively assist you in creating your long-term plans, evaluate your progress, and offer custom suggestions and wisdom for you and your family as your situation evolves over the course of your life.

As you collaborate with your wealth adviser and other advisers, keep in mind the need to revisit your thinking and your plans periodically. The world and the markets change, your family and financial circumstances will change, and your thinking on a range of matters will evolve. Schedule time a few times each year to "think about your thinking."

Congratulations on completing this book and choosing to organize your life and wealth intentionally rather than accepting what randomly comes your way. It is my hope that the Eight Points in book will guide you toward Financial Confidence in the years ahead.

EIGHT POINTS of FINANCIAL CONFIDENCE

Tax-Wise Strategies	Education Funding
Income-for-Life Planning	Wealth Transfer Planning
Reducing Risks of Financial Losses	Managing Wealth
Your Goals and Most Important Future Plans	Measuring and Monitoring Your Progress

Acknowledgments

Many talented people were important in the writing of this revised edition of *Eight Points.* I am honored to have so many colleagues who were willing to devote hours and hours and effort to this project. Though not a complete list, I wish to thank the following:

Larry Swedroe, my Buckingham colleague, prolific author, and mentor to me and many in the firm and the financial industry. Thank you for your recommendations, editing, and encouragement. Thank you also for writing the foreword to this edition.

Thanks to **Nicholas Ledden, Leslie Garrison**, and the compliance team at Buckingham for numerous reviews and improvements. Nick's incredible editing of my books and blog posts sound so much like "my voice" that I have a difficult time finding the recommended changes! Thank you all so much.

I met **Gerry Finnegan**, CFP®, on April 16, 1982, my first day in the industry. The first "fee-only" financial planner in my community, Gerry has provided extremely valuable technical edits and suggestions on this and each of the books I have written. Thank you, Gerry, for your time and attention and for your example of how to do it the right way!

Thanks to my "**Buck Lincoln**" colleagues for taking care of business when I was writing with my door closed and offering me encouragement and suggestions, all very important to getting this revision to the finish line.

Finally, to **Cris Trautner** and **Aaron Vacin**, my tireless editors, publishers, and enthusiastic supporters at Infusionmedia. Through a stroke of random luck, I met you, and together we have produced six books and revisions. Thank you for your countless hours and always valuable advice. Let's work on a new project soon!

ADDITIONAL BOOKS
BY JEFF C. JOHNSON

The Five Financial Foundations:
A Guide to Building a Better Future

The Five Financial Foundations were developed over 30 years of my career as a stockbroker, financial planner, and teacher. By observing real people who intuitively applied these basic principles, I was able to learn the simple secrets to working toward building a secure financial life. Best of all, I learned that these people almost always benefited in nonfinancial ways—less work and worry as life progressed, happy marriages and family situations, and a calm that is the result of having a sense of "Financial Confidence."

If you want a bigger and better future, if you want to be empowered and motivated to start building a firm financial foundation, if you want your stress over finances to be lower and your financial security to be higher, then this book is for you.

Available on Amazon.com and Jeffcjohnson.com.

The Extreme Retirement Planning
Workbook: Navigating the Next
30 Years (Second Edition)

When my grandfather retired from the local telephone company at age 65, he had pension income for life and Social Security retirement income. For the next 18 years, he had no reason to worry about money or his financial well-being.

Not true for many of today's prospective retirees, who have to learn to save, manage investments, arrange their income—and be sure it can last for 30 years or more!

The Extreme Retirement Planning Workbook was written to help Americans everywhere determine IF they should retire, HOW to arrange their assets and income streams, and WHEN retirement might be feasible.

If you're feeling like retirement today is uncertain (or maybe even a little scary), get a copy of *The Extreme Retirement Planning Workbook* and apply it to your situation.

Available on Amazon.com and Jeffcjohnson.com.